The Successful
ACADEMIC
LIBRARIAN

The Successful
ACADEMIC
LIBRARIAN

Winning Strategies From Library Leaders

Edited by
Gwen Meyer Gregory

 Information Today, Inc.
Medford, New Jersey

First printing, 2005

The Successful Academic Librarian:
Winning Strategies From Library Leaders

Copyright © 2005 by Gwen Meyer Gregory

Library of Congress Cataloging-in-Publication Data

The successful academic librarian: winning strategies from library leaders / edited by Gwen Meyer Gregory.
    p. cm.
    Includes bibliographical references and index.
    ISBN 1-57387-232-6
    1. Academic librarians--United States. 2. Academic librarians--Vocational guidance. 3. Academic librarians--Employment. I. Gregory, Gwen Meyer, 1965–
    Z682.4.C63S84 2005
    027.7'092--dc22

             2005017201

President and CEO: Thomas H. Hogan, Sr.
Editor-in-Chief and Publisher: John B. Bryans
Managing Editor: Amy M. Holmes
VP Graphics and Production: M. Heide Dengler
Book Designer: Kara Mia Jalkowski
Cover Designer: Michele Quinn
Copyeditor: Pat Hadley-Miller
Proofreader: Mary Ainsworth
Indexer: Enid L. Zafran

Dedication

To Anne Morgan, Jim Hemesath, Chuck Baldonado,
and the other academic librarians who mentored me
and helped me become the librarian I am today.

Contents

PART 1: THE BASICS—GETTING OFF TO A GOOD START

CHAPTER 1

Start at the Beginning—Your Job Responsibilities and How to Accomplish Them 3
Rebecca Miller with Nancy Sosna Bohm

CHAPTER 2

Building Strong Collaborative Relationships with Disciplinary Faculty 13
Elizabeth O. Hutchins

CHAPTER 3

Building the Profession—Research, Creative Activities, and Publication by Academic Librarians 31
Joan Beam and Cathy Cranston

CHAPTER 7

Verla J. Peterson

CHAPTER 8

Kris Swank

PART 3: TALES FROM THE TRENCHES—ACADEMIC LIBRARIANS SHARE THEIR STORIES

CHAPTER 12

Notes From a Cataloger—Success in Technical Services **157**
Wendy Baia

CHAPTER 13

Witches Brew or Gourmet Gumbo—Tenure in the Library **171**
Molly E. Molloy

CHAPTER 14

**Moving to the Academy in Mid-Career—A Field Guide
for the Experienced Librarian** **183**
Anna Gold

CHAPTER 15
A View From the Top—What the Director or Dean
Is Looking For 199
Benjamin Wakashige and Emily Asch

Preface

Why am I an academic librarian?

I've been a public librarian, I have my K–12 school library certification and I have worked in a variety of graduate programs as a library educator. So why have I been an academic librarian for the last twenty-plus years? I don't know if I can say for sure. I do know, however, that when I wanted to return to my home town, I asked a variety of people where I should work and they all said that the place where the most exciting things were happening was the community college library. I remember hearing "growth and expansion," "automation and technology" "risk-taking," "diverse clientele," "fast-moving" and "teaching and learning" and I guess I was sold. I thought it might be my match. And they weren't wrong. From the beginning it was a ride with as many ups as downs and as much chaotic change as solid progress. We grew faster than the speed of light, automated everything we could, took risks whenever we could – usually to attract the administration's attention, served a diverse clientele of adults and then ventured out to serve special needs K–12 kids in an experimental public/academic and school facility, and, through it all, struggled to maintain our presence in the classroom and to promote the library as a teaching and learning center.

I'm a firm believer in stressing to individuals as they search for their first job or their next job or their mid-career change in the profession that they need to find their match. The match has to provide ongoing personal and professional satisfaction; the match has to be intellectually stimulating; the match has to bring enjoyment. The last two decades have been great fun. I'm not saying I've had more fun than public librarians or school librarians but I'm saying it's been a great match. I've had the best staff in the world and we seem to have had it all: faculty status, extensive integrated information literacy, broad staff development opportunities, incredible relationships with classroom faculty, mentoring new librarians and broadening responsibilities for mid-career professionals. Not without a great deal of work, but a self-defined learning organization—the stuff higher education "is made of"—often makes it more possible.

So why choose an academic environment for your match? Although all librarians teach their patrons, academic librarians:

- experience in-depth teaching and learning enrichment for curriculum support;

- play a pivotal role in the real life consequences of teaching, learning and using information such as designing and delivering critical thinking assignments for nursing students or assisting a student in designing a business plan for their first small business;

- work in collegial work groups or teams;

- often have more flexible work environments and schedules; and,

- have opportunities for research and reflection on the profession.

For some, it's the perfect match!

So, in making up your mind ... should I start out in "the academy?" "Did I make the right choice?" "Should I change careers?" ...you will want to get other perspectives on academic career issues and read further to make up your mind. While some chapters offer stories, opinions and facts on ongoing library issues, other chapters provide new information for academic librarians on interviewing and getting that perfect job as well as mid-career job shifts, mentoring and a particularly in-depth and interesting chapter on service commitment for the academic. Learn and enjoy.

Acknowledgments

All the contributors to this book deserve thanks for their hard work and creative efforts. Academic librarians will profit from hearing the viewpoints of their many colleagues. These authors stepped right up to the plate and shared their thoughts, opinions, and experiences. Other colleagues, including Carol Dickerson, Rachel Singer Gordon, Donnelyn Curtis, Steve Lawson, Sarah Nesbeitt Johnson, Karl Henson, and Doug Suarez provided the editor with encouragement and assistance. Everyone at the Tutt Library of Colorado College has been supportive. Erika Lenz has helped improve my writing immeasurably over the past decade or so.

The staff at Information Today, Inc. has worked with me through the years on my articles and book reviews and now on this book. John Bryans encouraged me to undertake the project and provided important feedback. Amy Holmes did a great job steering the book through the editorial and production process.

None of this would have been possible without the support of my husband, Don Meyer, and the rest of my family. Thanks for cheering me on!

Introduction

"I have always imagined that Paradise will be a kind of library."
—Jorge Luis Borges (1899–1986)

People find careers in academic libraries in many ways. You may have gone right from undergraduate school to library school and straight to a university library career. You may have had many other jobs or careers before choosing libraries, or worked as a library paraprofessional before deciding to go for a master's degree in Library Science. You may even have professional library experience in special or public libraries but are new to academia. Regardless of your background, if you are heading for a career as an academic librarian there are many things you need to know. This book will give you a head start.

Libraries have been part of higher education for hundreds of years. European universities began in the twelfth century, but their book collections were small. As printing grew and more books became available in the sixteenth century, these libraries began to expand. In the United States, the earliest college librarians were instructors or tutors at their institutions, with care of the library tacked on to their jobs. During the nineteenth century, professors or college administrators often did double duty running the library. However, it is notable that having a library was considered essential for an institution of higher education. Toward the end of that century, the profession of librarianship emerged: In 1876, the American Library Association was founded, and in 1887 Melvil Dewey started the School of Library Economy at Columbia College in New York City. As the profession developed, so did college libraries. Collection size, number of staff members, and services provided increased throughout the twentieth century. The growth of graduate study and faculty research after World War II put new demands on library resources. Currently, librarians are a valued part of the campus community, managing access to electronic resources and teaching Internet research while still providing more traditional services.

As you begin work in higher education, think of constructing your career as a process, like building a house. You need to do many things along the way to complete the house. Your academic preparation, including undergraduate and graduate education, is the solid foundation on which all is based. You frame out the structure with your particular skills, perhaps specializing in reference or in cataloging. Over time, you put up the walls as you flesh out your career experience with different tasks and jobs. You link to your colleagues on and off campus, just as the house links to water, electricity, and other utilities. As the structure grows and takes shape, you add features like windows and doors, just as you add publications and service to your librarianship activities. Of course, you will not finish building your career for many years. It will grow and change as you do. As your interests change, you may take new directions in your career, like building an addition to your house as a family grows. Your goal is to end up with a comfortable and successful home (or career).

I was inspired to write this book by my desire to help academic librarians build flourishing careers while reducing the stresses inherent in our profession. I knew that many of my colleagues could share valuable advice, so after creating an outline I asked other academic librarians to contribute chapters. The authors work at many institutions of higher education, from community colleges to research universities. They are recent graduates and librarians with decades of experience. They work and live in different regions of the U.S. and Canada. Here they have a common goal: to help other academic librarians succeed. Each has thought long and hard about their chosen topic, and they sincerely hope to help you be a better academic librarian. Many also want to help you avoid pitfalls and problems they have encountered in their careers and to point out shortcuts to academic prosperity.

As with any book made up of contributed pieces, there are differences in style between the chapters. Several authors interviewed other librarians and include quotes in their chapters. Other authors take a more scholarly approach to their topics, with descriptions of research and extensive bibliographies. You may even find disagreement among the authors on some academic library issues. This is a reflection of the diversity of the profession; we all have our own ideas and opinions—all of them valid and, as I hope you'll agree, worthwhile hearing.

The Successful Academic Librarian is arranged into three major parts, with each chapter covering a different aspect of the work of the academic librarian. The first part, "The Basics—Getting Off to a Good Start," will help you understand the pieces of an academic library job.

It includes a discussion of faculty status for librarians as well as chapters on accomplishing your job responsibilities, working with faculty, getting published, and performing service. The second part gives you "Things to Think About—Getting and Keeping a Great Job." Here you will find tips on interviewing, having mentors, dealing with unions, receiving continuing education, and documenting your work. In the third part, "Tales from the Trenches—Academic Librarians Share Their Stories," experienced librarians tell you about their careers. You hear from a nontenure-track librarian, a faculty librarian, and a librarian who joined academia after working in other types of libraries for many years. Finally, a library director shares his thoughts on the qualities an academic librarian needs to succeed.

This is not meant to be a research study of academic librarianship, but rather a readable guidebook. As your colleagues, we want you to succeed.

Welcome to academia!

Works Cited

Budd, John. *The Academic Library: Its Context, Its Purpose, and Its Operation.* Englewood, CO: Libraries Unlimited, 1998.

Jefferson, George, and G. C. K. Smith-Burnett, Eds. *The College Library: A Collection of Essays.* London: Clive Bingley, 1978.

Lyle, Guy R. *The Administration of the College Library.* New York: H. W. Wilson, 1944.

Part 1

The Basics—Getting Off to a Good Start

CHAPTER 1

Start at the Beginning—
Your Job Responsibilities and
How to Accomplish Them

Rebecca Miller with Nancy Sosna Bohm

*"Work is either fun or drudgery. It depends on your
attitude. I like fun."*
—Colleen C. Barrett

A colleague and I once taught a class where we used librarian
stereotypes as a search example. We thought it would be fun to dress
up as stereotypical librarians, so we put our hair in buns and wore
glasses, long skirts, and high-collared blouses. To our chagrin, when
we arrived in the classroom, no one noticed anything different about
our appearance. We realized that we must fit that popular image too
well on an average day.

Although I may look the part of a librarian, when I began my first
faculty librarian job, I was nervous about my ability to actually
accomplish my responsibilities. Would I meet expectations? The first
big challenge I faced was fitting into the culture, learning how the system worked, and developing good relationships with people. I soon
realized that I also needed to organize my time and duties so that I
could accomplish them. Even now that I have become comfortable in
my role, I still continually re-evaluate my skills and decide if I need to
make any changes in how I fulfill my duties. Along the way, I have
learned many techniques and strategies.

Working with Others—You're Not Alone

Getting along with your supervisor, coworkers, support staff, and student assistants is a critical part of your job. Become acquainted with other individuals' personalities and backgrounds. Learning the idiosyncrasies of your work environment will allow you to stay within the norms of the library culture. For example, each library has its own acceptable noise level. If you are the loudest one in the library, some will find you abrasive, whereas if you are the quietest one, you may be overlooked.

Meeting your supervisor's expectations is a priority, so you need to determine your supervisor's personality and style of leadership. A supervisor with a hands-on approach will wish to be involved in all decisions and apprised of every development. If your supervisor is more hands-off, you can use your own discretion as to whether your superior needs to be consulted. Supervisors' social styles may also vary along a continuum from being best friends to maintaining a professional relationship. It is your responsibility as the employee to fit into the supervisor's style. Regardless of managerial style, eventually you will have either a formal or an informal evaluation. It is easy to get defensive and anxious when receiving comments or criticism. Remember that your supervisor is giving you valuable feedback, which can help you improve job performance.

It is also beneficial to recognize coworkers' styles and attempt to mesh with them. A new librarian will need to be alert to both the personalities and territories of colleagues in order to avoid inadvertently offending anyone. Coworkers who have a long history with the institution may feel threatened by newcomers, or need time to adjust to the addition of an unfamiliar member to the library team. Generally, the time to suggest changes is after fitting into the culture of the library. Be willing to learn from experienced coworkers, both professional librarians and the support staff. They will appreciate your respect for their experience. Collaborating with colleagues on day-to-day tasks and special projects increases the total available expertise and creativity you can draw on. As an example, this chapter was much easier to write with two authors working on it.

Take advantage of opportunities to get to know others and allow your coworkers to discover what you have to offer the library. Serving on library committees brings together people from different areas and increases your awareness of activities outside your own department.

Although meetings can sometimes seem long and fruitless, they are still a chance to socialize with colleagues. Do not be afraid to spend some time socializing, so long as it does not interfere with your ability to accomplish your assigned duties. Casual conversation is a way to build relationships, which allow for better work collaboration. However, be very careful about participating in negative gossip and complaining, which can breed a climate of distrust. If you look over your shoulder to see who is entering the room, that is a sign the conversation should be abandoned.

It is also important to maintain a positive attitude in order to be a good example to those you supervise. Even if supervising is not in your job description, it is likely that you will at least supervise student workers. You need to have realistic expectations about what student library assistants can accomplish. One librarian had the experience of students moving the serials collection and putting them in order backwards. Students may only work a few hours a week, and they also have to attend classes, and write papers, thus the library job is often not their highest priority. Nevertheless, you can use them to complete work for which you are ultimately responsible. Therefore, if you have assigned a lengthy or complicated task, be sure to check the student's progress early and often, especially if it is a new student employee or there is a language barrier to overcome. Because of the high turnover of student assistants, written and very specific procedures for common tasks can minimize the time you spend training them.

Supervising full-time staff is quite different. They are generally more committed to their jobs and share responsibility for the quality of the completed tasks. When problems do arise, they should be addressed immediately in a nonthreatening manner, perhaps using humor for minor issues. Focus on the work-related behaviors affected by an individual's habits or personality traits rather than on personal flaws. If possible, suggest how to perform the task more effectively or brainstorm a solution together. Regardless of whom you are supervising, make an effort to give more affirming than negative comments. Clarity is always essential, especially if there is a diversity of languages in the workplace. I encourage my subordinates to talk to me or send me e-mail with any procedural or policy questions so that I will not be surprised by the outcome of their work.

Individuals outside the library can also be crucial to the successful completion of your projects. Your job requires that you interact with professors, administrators, and others at the college. At times, I have carried a small notebook to record names, roles, and even physical descriptions of various faculty and staff. If you are able to hail someone by name, you demonstrate that you recognize that person's unique value. This applies to students as well as colleagues.

Try to get to know how your campus works, including the hierarchy of the administration and its procedures. Colleagues and other staff can be a good source of information on where to go with a particular question. When I first came to work, I frequently asked one of the support staff members about campus procedures. She had been there for many years and understood many unspoken rules of our college's administration. Determine whether the administration tends to have formal or more laissez-faire policies. You might need to find out, for example, what criteria are used to determine budgetary increases for your department or the library as a whole. Try to avoid asking for special exceptions to rules and procedures. Sometimes I have been able to determine the accepted route to circumventing the customary procedure. For example, I have negotiated to borrow student assistants from a less busy area instead of requesting to hire more students. Remember that the administrative office staff members are individuals, many of whom are willing to help you accomplish your goals for the benefit of the institution as a whole.

You will come across many unique characters that inhabit the academic realm. I have learned to weather the tirades of professors who take personal offense when the library cannot meet their demands. There is one professor who used to become so upset that his face turned red and veins stood out in his neck. I have learned to identify the difficult people, and try to be prepared to meet them with both extra diplomacy and firmness. Try to find some common ground or empathize with their frustrations without letting the conversation degenerate into a pity party or criticism of the institution. Occasionally I have been able to befriend difficult people by initiating small talk. This demonstrated to them that I did not take their temperaments personally, and I valued them as human beings. I have even been able to then collaborate with them on worthwhile projects, which mutually increases our value to the institution.

You are more likely to have a good working relationship with professors if they recognize you as a worthy colleague. I am ready to assist them in a variety of ways, whether it is with their personal research, bibliographic instruction for their students, or creating a Web page for a class. When I have built working relationships with them in these settings, it is easier to approach them about increased collaboration. I recently worked extensively with new Communications faculty members on their personal research, which opened the door for me to work with them on integrating information literacy into the Communications curriculum. Serving on committees, attending meetings, and going to campus events are ways of establishing yourself as a familiar colleague in the minds of professors. When talking with them, be careful about using library jargon that may be confusing to them. Once I told a professor that I would be doing a lot of weeding during the summer. He looked confused and asked if I had a summer job doing landscaping. I had to keep a straight face and tactfully explain that "weeding" referred to removing old books from the collection.

It is also important to respect the technology, custodial, and other university staff, without whom the library would be a much less pleasant place to work. Be considerate of the demands on their time; often they have many different people clamoring for attention. Attempt to troubleshoot minor technology glitches yourself, and when reporting a problem, provide a list of what you have tried. When I have organized events in the library that are likely to leave a mess, I have enlisted student assistants to do some of the cleanup and warned the custodians in advance. I regularly greet the custodial staff and acknowledge what they do. Developing friendly relationships can make a better working experience for all.

Managing Your Job Duties—A Time for Everything

While I was learning to fit into the system, I also needed to establish my own personal routine. I began by determining my goals and objectives. These included both short-term and long-term plans, from prioritizing my everyday activities to considering my professional future.

When organizing your schedule, begin by making a list of your duties. These may change as you discover tasks that were not defined in your job description but that do fall into your area of responsibility. Prioritize your job duties both by deadlines and by importance. You can determine importance by looking at how the project affects the students and faculty, your supervisor, or your professional development. To illustrate, I once discovered that a different page had accidentally replaced the library home page, and I immediately dropped everything else to fix it. In contrast, weeding is typically not as urgent, and I tend to put it off until I have spare time in the summer and during holidays.

If your position is tenure track and your institution places a high emphasis on publishing, that should be near the top of your list of priorities. However, some institutions require you to concentrate preferentially on your librarian duties in order to attain tenure. You should become familiar with your institution's tenure requirements and plan accordingly. You may also want to plan projects that help you to develop professionally. For example, serving on national or regional library committees can be rewarding and can help to raise your standing in the profession.

When you have decided on the priority of your tasks, plan the best times to work on them. Find out the expectations for your schedule, whether you need to work strictly in the library from nine to five or if you can sometimes work from home. Schedule projects that require a high level of concentration for times when you are less likely to be interrupted—I avoid working on detail-oriented projects when I'm on the reference desk, as I know I'll be called on to answer any number of student questions. Understanding the cycle of the academic year can also help your planning. During busy times of the semester, you may need to postpone lower priority tasks. Use summers and break times to catch up on these tasks. Use a planner to schedule future projects so they will not be forgotten. Find a scheduling method that works best for you, and make good use of it. One day, my supervisor asked if I was busy. I said that I was not, but only later thought to check my calendar. I discovered I was supposed to be in a conference downtown that day, and I had to run for the train. Since then, I have become more conscientious about using my planner.

You will want to organize your workspace and projects so that you can easily leave and then return to them. For example, I lost an important paper for a project because I had not straightened up my desk in a long time. Having several files for papers of various degrees of importance can help prevent such mishaps. Computer files also need to be organized and regularly cleaned up. If I know I'm likely to be interrupted, I save relevant documents onto a file server or e-mail them to myself so I can access them from other computers at a later time, being sure to name the files logically to avoid confusion.

As you are beginning your job, you will need to master basic procedures. Your supervisor may only have the time to give you a rudimentary introduction to your tasks. Be sure to ask questions as you go along if you need clarification. If there is no manual, you might want to fill a notebook with your own list of procedures. It is a good idea to do a self-evaluation of your skills periodically and see if you could use improvements. For example, when I first began my job, I felt uncomfortable doing instruction, which is one of my job duties. So I made an effort to read books, attend workshops and conferences, and get advice from colleagues who are more experienced instructors.

You will also need to update your technology skills constantly. The more experience you have learning to use new technology, the easier it will be to figure out the latest innovations. Your life will be easier if you can embrace change. I was not initially happy when I discovered my new job would require me to use a Macintosh, but I quickly realized it would be a good opportunity to become proficient on a different type of computer. However, you should not push for change unnecessarily. It is easy to be dazzled by the latest technology, but consider other factors, such as cost and long-term usefulness. Listservs can keep you up-to-date about the value of new advances in technology. Become familiar with the technology within your institution, such as networks, printers, software, and Web sites. This will allow you to speak intelligently to your information technology department.

While managing your day-to-day tasks and staying up-to-date, you will also need to manage the stress that comes with handling the competing demands on your time. Make sure you have periods of rest. It is best if you can leave your work when you go home, and use that time for relaxation and family. If you are doing professional development activities outside of work, try to keep these contained to a set period of time, perhaps an hour each evening, so they do not spread into your entire life. During your off-times, try to engage in activities that are different from your work activities. I try to avoid using the computer at home given that I use it all day at work. Similarly, if I am sitting at the desk for long periods, I will try to go for walks during my breaks. When I maintain a healthy lifestyle, it helps me think clearly and give my optimal performance.

In addition to managing your own job pressures, you may also need to help others cope with their stress. This is especially true in an academic setting where you may be working with students anxious about research papers, professors worried about tenure, and coworkers with heavy workloads. As a librarian, listening to the information needs of others is already part of your job. Taking a few minutes to hear a student bemoan a noisy roommate or financial woes is not far removed from your assigned role.

Even as you try to be organized, remember that all things connected to the library are subject to change. Your carefully planned schedules and procedures need to have flexibility built into them. This will make you more available to meet unexpected requests and needs of library users.

Fulfilling Your Job Role—Serving Up Information

As you master your daily job duties, you will be free to focus on the mission of serving your academic community. You may work in public or technical services, but the primary purpose for all your activities is still to make sure that the students and faculty of the university receive the library services they need.

Circulation librarians put a face on the library. When I worked in circulation, I made an effort to impart an ethic of service to the employees who worked in my department. Have clear, updated procedures and answers to frequently asked questions available at the front desk. Be attentive to ways the procedures can be modified to streamline circulation tasks for both the staff and the patrons. When a patron comes in with a problem you can easily solve by harmlessly bending a policy, do not be a stickler for the rules. Evaluate statistics of library use and listen to library staff and clientele. Most importantly, show respect for the public you serve.

Reference is also a front line for serving the public. At the reference desk, be warm and welcoming. Many people have stereotypes of stern and intimidating librarians, which can be a barrier to asking for help. In contrast, I try to show a willingness to help and an interest in their topics in order to reduce those barriers. Be prepared to spend plenty of time with a student researching a difficult topic for a lengthy paper. Frequently students tell the professor how helpful a certain librarian was, and the professor may notice that the quality of their sources is markedly better than in the past. Consult other librarians if they have more experience than you have in a particular subject area. Be careful never to laugh at what a student may ask or tell you. A student once came up to me and congratulated me on winning the

Pulitzer Prize. I assumed she was joking so I laughed. The student looked very embarrassed and left quickly. I later discovered there was an award-winning author with my name, and the student honestly thought that I was her.

Bibliographic instruction continues to gain in importance at academic institutions. Information has become increasingly accessible, but requires more skill to locate, select, and use. The information fluency techniques we teach can be helpful throughout the student's life. You cannot usually cover everything during the time allotted to you. Lately, I have been attempting to focus less on specific techniques of using individual databases. Instead of just giving them "click here" instructions, I now try to cover broader principles such as how to evaluate sources. This is especially important because students often find much of their information online and are not necessarily critical about what they select. Additionally, I have learned to expect the unexpected during instruction sessions. In spite of having prepared handouts and Web sites galore, I have often been foiled by a failed Internet connection and have had to improvise. With practice, you can pull this off with grace.

Technical services librarians also need to keep the end user in mind, and work to make entries and services as useful as possible. This could include adding table of contents notes or local subject headings for items frequently used for a specialized area of the curriculum of your school. Even if you have cataloging quotas to meet, these additions to the catalog records increase the value of your work. The ebb and flow of the acquisitions of your library will be tied to the fiscal year, so learn the patterns and try to make them mesh with the demands of the academic cycles. To the extent of your ability to orchestrate the department, be sure processing of new items will not be held up by the lack of supplies or staff, especially at critical times in the semester. As in the public services departments, model an attitude of concern for the needs of the patrons, rather than complaining about the work they generate. Your contributions to the library collections are a valuable resource for library users.

Library Web sites have increasingly become a vehicle for serving the information needs of library users. Many current students do not enter the physical library at all, preferring to use the library Web pages from their dorm rooms. This means the Web pages must be easy for them to use without much assistance. I work with faculty to develop Web pages for specific classes. I also observe first-hand how students use the pages. I then see where they have problems and can alter the layout or links accordingly. In general, I avoid lengthy areas of text on the main pages, and organize the content for maximum use and clarity. Consider that the Web page is often the first contact with the library that prospective and new students have.

You Do Make a Difference

I initially entered library work because it is a service profession. I felt a desire to help others learn from and gain access to the wealth of information available today. Sometimes this goal can become lost in the midst of my day-to-day job duties. However, I have discovered some techniques to help me keep my focus on service. Maintaining good relationships with others and effectively organizing my tasks frees me from many worries. In addition, as I am performing my job functions, I try to remember what should ideally motivate me—meeting the information needs of the students, faculty, and other patrons of my library.

You never know how the work you do could have a long-lasting impact on other's lives. Early one spring semester, a senior asked at the reference desk for a list of classes that still had open slots. After further conversation, it turned out that he was considering dropping out of school, and the library was his last resort. I spent the next two hours helping him research the classes that fulfilled requirements he needed. At the end of the semester, as the students filed past during the graduation ceremony, this student saluted me. Suddenly it all seemed worthwhile.

Special thanks for the input from the librarians of Lake Forest College and Sarah Park of Northwest Missouri State University.

CHAPTER 2

Building Strong Collaborative Relationships with Disciplinary Faculty

Elizabeth O. Hutchins

"A teacher affects eternity; he can never tell where his influence stops."
—Henry Adams (1838–1918)

In a climate of rapidly expanding information horizons, successful teaching and learning in higher education depends upon building strong collaborative relationships between librarians and faculty in other disciplines. How does one establish these relationships, what are the challenges, and what is the role of entry-level academic librarians? These are some of the questions this chapter will focus on by examining the cultural climate of higher education, exploring librarians' professional expertise, and identifying strategic opportunities.

Cross-Cultural Understandings … and Misunderstandings

Launching a career in academic librarianship is not unlike planning a move to a foreign country. Although culture shock is expected, it is a good idea to learn as much as one can about those who inhabit this new land. Academic librarians need to frame their partnerships within the larger context of the institution's mission, the expectations and assumptions of teaching faculty, and the library's program.

Successful collaboration with teaching faculty is all about relationships. Working with faculty can be challenging because the areas of expertise that librarians bring to this partnership are often misunderstood if not invisible. Where then does one start? Initially it is helpful to identify some essential characteristics of your institution: Is it a large university, small liberal arts college, community college, or vocational institute? How large is the enrollment? What is the profile of the student body? Is the tenure and promotion system alive and well? Are undergraduate classes predominantly lecture oriented or is there a pedagogical shift away from teacher centered instruction to student centered, resource-based learning (Barr and Tagg, p. 12)? Perhaps these are all stereotypes with the truth existing somewhere in between. Whatever the case, a librarian needs to be aware of the institution's culture, faculty/student composition, mission, and key initiatives (Iannuzzi, p. 98).

Then there is the library culture. What are the library's mission and goals? In what way do they serve the college's mission? Is the library primarily a teaching library with significant course related/integrated instruction or is it a research library that offers online tutorials, information literacy workshops, or courses for credit, all of which may require little faculty collaboration? Is information literacy a priority? Do librarians have faculty status? These questions are important for they influence the faculty's view of librarians and the librarians' opportunities for collaboration with teaching faculty.

Now to get back to culture shock. Why culture shock? Isn't an academic setting precisely where you have been immersed for a number of years during your undergraduate and graduate studies? Yes, and this is why as an entry-level librarian you may experience shock. The relationship you have had with faculty changes when you return to campus as a professional. You are now supposed to be a peer, yet you may not feel like one. Even though one's credibility in the eyes of the faculty may be enhanced by faculty status or perhaps by a second master's degree, an entry-level librarian may still lack confidence in being perceived as a peer and even in acting as a peer. These feelings are to be expected as you become acculturated to this new community of scholars, but unfortunately as an entry-level academic librarian you probably have not received the same training or recognition as beginning teaching faculty have when procuring their terminal degrees.

In most institutions of higher education, academic freedom, the tenure system, and distinctions between faculty and staff all play a key role in the cultural climate, a setting that is often distinguished by significant power differentials. Of course, new faculty members have qualms about legitimacy as they begin their professional journeys. However, the academic hoops they jump through in procuring their Ph.D.s are also ones of acculturation where they delve deeply into scholarly research, are socialized into the publish-or-perish environment, accept the hierarchical nature of the tenure system while they also strive to be part of it, and procure mentors. This process includes specialization in a disciplinary content area, original research, and ongoing assessment. Simply put, it imbues them with a common set of values and "a state of mind that ... is a commitment to a transcendent academic culture, to an intellectual community, and to the pursuit of inquiry" (Mitchell and Morton, p. 380). Once faculty members have achieved their goal, they embrace both its responsibilities and rights.

Academic librarians, on the other hand, are socialized into a service-oriented model "that pervades library education ... [and] severely handicaps librarians who will eventually find themselves assuming positions where the collegiality of academic peer relationships with nonlibrary faculty is an expected norm" (Mitchell and Morton, p. 384). In contrast to their faculty colleagues who focus on an area of disciplinary specialty, librarians are usually generalists with wide interdisciplinary knowledge: "Librarians and faculty identify a disconnection that keeps the two separated, but only librarians view this disconnection as problematic" (Christiansen, Stombler, and Thaxton, p. 116). In addition, they frequently prefer to "function in partnership with, and in support of, the teaching goals of all campus units, not in typical academic isolation from their colleagues in other departments" (Haynes, p. 191). Simply put, teaching faculty and academic librarians have different priorities and areas of expertise. Although the teaching faculty are committed to having students adept at the terminology and theoretical foundation of their particular discipline, librarians' instructional expertise resides more in process, pedagogy, critical thinking, and research strategies that focus on having students become life-long learners skilled in accessing a broad range of information.

So how do faculty view librarians? One often discovers that faculty talk about the library rather than librarians. Those who care about libraries are frequently more interested in the library's scholarly resources, how the collection is developed, online databases, and journal subscriptions than the library's instructional program. In fact, faculty may be unaware of the expertise of those who make these resources available and teach students how to access them. In addition, given that faculty researchers rely on an in-depth knowledge of their specialization and a network of scholars, they may not realize that students *need* instruction in library research.

Many teaching faculty admire the work librarians do, but there are others who may have a number of assumptions embedded in their consultation with librarians. For example, faculty may think that: "(1) librarians are generally nice people who are there to help, particularly with technical questions about how various kinds of retrieval processes work, … (2) researchers probably will not need them very much because they already have an idea of what kinds of material they need to find; however, (3) librarians are there if researchers run into trouble" (Leckie, p. 205). Although faculty view librarians as professionals, they are frequently seen more as persons engaged in a helpful service role rather than as academic equals. Entry-level librarians need to be aware of these assumptions because when they feel a lack of credibility vis-à-vis the faculty with whom they wish to develop working relationships, it may not be merely because they are new to academic librarianship but also because of the way in which academic librarianship is perceived—or misperceived. It is important to have an understanding of the distinctions that exist between librarians and teaching faculty.

We Too Have Disciplinary Expertise!

Understanding and embracing the expertise we offer to partnerships with teaching faculty is fundamental to viewing ourselves, and being viewed by others, as colleagues and educators. It is also essential to the role we play in supporting and enhancing our institution's academic program. What distinguishes librarians' disciplinary expertise? Some areas of specialization include information literacy, the organization of access to resources, the dissemination of knowledge, and facilitating users' connection to key scholarly conversations. As Leckie and Fullerton note, "Since most librarians cannot claim that they do the kinds of original research conducted by the faculty, it is even more imperative that they be able to demonstrate that they do contribute to pedagogy" (Leckie and Fullerton, p. 6). For example, librarians' expertise in research strategies and critical thinking processes directly link with the teaching faculty's priorities.

Barbara Fister noted in an e-mail communication that faculty colleagues at Gustavus Adolphus College participated in library-run information literacy workshops because they believed that information literacy is "not about technology, it's about pedagogy."

Mitchell and Morton recommend that "rather than thinking passively of librarianship as the organizing and retrieving of knowledge, librarians should think of it in dynamic terms: assembling knowledge, creating pathways and gateways to knowledge, and providing introductions to knowledge or to the pathway and gateways" (Mitchell and Morton, p. 10). Janet Swan Hill, in maintaining that librarianship is an academic discipline, notes that "[b]ecause many librarians' assignments involve them in service to another discipline (e.g., "music librarian" or "medical librarian"), nonlibrarians may be deceived into believing that the librarianship portion of the job is the adjunct rather than the disciplinary specialty. It may be easy to slip into thinking of these "[modifier]-librarians" in terms of what they are not (e.g., not really musicologists) instead of what they are (librarians), but such interpretation is both incorrect and inappropriate" (Hill, p. 72).

So, what are academic librarians? We are knowledge builders and experts at tapping into scholarly conversations. When students enter college, they are joining a community of inquiry. Connecting with scholarly dialogue is at the heart of their learning, as well as faculty research and academic librarians' vocation. Ernest Boyer celebrated the disciplinary expertise of librarians. In 1987, he said, "Those in charge of information services on a campus are the renaissance people who are able to guide students through the typology of knowledge and help them discover the relationships that no single department and no single professor can provide" (Brevik, p. 46). With support such as Boyer's, it is imperative that academic librarians promote their disciplinary expertise as one that is both complementary and integral to that of learning and teaching in higher education. For example, librarians' expertise in organizing, evaluating, and providing access to information enhances the teaching, research, and curriculum needs of different disciplines precisely because collection development and cataloging librarians have a thorough knowledge of these areas. Making the resources available depends, in turn, on extraordinary proficiency in systems, Web design, and instruction. Although not readily visible to faculty or students, a wide spectrum of expertise among academic librarians (ranging from catalogers and systems librarians to those engaged in reference and instruction) plays a key educational role in complementing the teaching faculty's disciplinary specialties.

In addition, although teaching faculty may be fully aware of the scholarly standards and expectations in their field, who except librarians are aware of the standards guiding information literacy, cataloging, and the growing field of digitization? Moreover, although the network of scholars is widely accepted as integral to teaching faculty's research, to what extent is it known that this research depends on parallel "bibliographic networks, authority control cooperatives, interlibrary loan consortia, library automation groups, and professional associations?" (Hill, p. 73). Clearly, librarians need to do a better job at marketing.

Why belabor the question of whether librarians' have their own area of disciplinary expertise? Because it is of the utmost importance that our expertise with information access, evaluation, and retrieval is understood as integral to supporting learning, teaching, research, and a strong culture of inquiry. Librarians and faculty have similar goals, namely to engage students in critical thinking, discipline-oriented learning that depends on the organization of knowledge, and an understanding of disciplinary and interdisciplinary discourses.

With information literacy of increasing importance, the time is ripe for academic librarians to collaborate with faculty in teaching students research and critical thinking skills. Snavely and Cooper identify a number of reasons why this would be a natural partnership:

- Information literacy goals match the mission of higher education to prepare graduates for life-long learning.

- An information literacy program complements and supports other programs in that finding, evaluating, and using information resources is at the heart of research.

- Information literacy provides students and faculty with the tools to handle a rapidly expanding world of information. (Snavely and Cooper, p. 56)

There are a number of more specific factors that contribute to this being an opportune time for library/faculty collaboration: students' increased—and at times indiscriminate—use of the Web, concerns about plagiarism and copyright issues, blurred distinction on the part of the users between Internet resources and proprietary online databases, availability of citation management software, wired class-rooms that allow for hands-on research instruction, the ongoing need to evaluate the credibility of popular and scholarly resources, rapidly expanding technology, departmental/curricular reviews, expanded faculty work loads, and an increased focus on assessment. In April 2004, Esther Grassian sent out an informal query of ILI-Listserv users requesting feedback on whether "college and university faculty have been turning to librarians more and more for help in teaching undergraduates information research and general critical thinking skills, as well as plagiarism avoidance and the concept of intellectual property." In her summary report dated May 5, 2004, she reported that she received twenty-one replies with sixteen in strong agreement, one seeing a slight trend, one who did not agree, and three who did not offer an opinion. Many respondents specifically mentioned a number of the factors identified in this article. Given these concerns, librarians may be well situated to collaborate with faculty in weaving research and critical thinking skills into courses (Rader, p. 74).

Clearly, information literacy strongly affirms the goals of the teaching faculty. However, for librarians, credibility as a teacher goes beyond proclaiming one's expertise and credentials. It involves live encounters with students and faculty. Yes, teaching can be intimidating if you have never been in this position. However, if you take the risk of allowing your energy to show, of sharing passion, and of being fully engaged in a classroom, you will discover that students will risk exploring questions with meaning for them. Why? Because they will trust you. Establishing trusting, authentic relationships is at the core of teaching and learning (Hutchins, p. 105). Regardless of how one organizes a class, students and faculty appreciate an energized experience that directly addresses the questions they are asking. If it does, they become genuinely involved in the research process, which usually creates a better product. Such engaged teaching and learning often results in a rewarding partnership among the students, faculty member, and librarian.

Becoming engaged and effective teachers takes both courage and practice. How does one do this? Having a mentor, inviting a colleague to observe a class, observing theirs, establishing a peer coaching relationship, attending workshops, or enrolling in the ACRL Institute for Information Literacy all offer good opportunities for enhancing our teaching expertise. If librarians can move beyond teaching skills and risk engaging students in critical thinking, we will actively contribute to pedagogy. This, in turn, will give us credibility and provide a foundation for partnership.

Strategic Opportunities and Challenges

Now ... how do we start working with teaching faculty?

Establishing an initial connection with a faculty member or with departments often depends on the librarian's outreach. One of the most successful approaches has been to start at the grass roots level with individual faculty members. Many faculty members do not know what services the library offers beyond that of collection development. Nor do they know whom to contact in the library to work with their particular area of expertise or their students. If your library already has a formal liaison program linking specific consulting librarians with departments, a framework for communication is clearly established. This gives both faculty and librarians permission to initiate contact.

Before contacting faculty, the librarian needs to do more digging, this time into the cultural context of the departments with which they will be working. Who are the stakeholders? What is their territory? How are they organized? How do they conduct research? How do they use the library? Which courses do they offer? How do they teach their courses?

It may be helpful to be aware of the different types of faculty. The distinctions between program directors, department chairs, full-time tenured or tenure track faculty, adjunct faculty, and lecturers are often important as each may have a different personal stake in the curriculum and the institution as a whole. Each also holds a different degree of power depending on the campus culture. For example, even though at a smaller liberal arts college faculty may resist hierarchical initiatives, at a large university getting the "buy-in" of program directors before connecting with individual faculty can play a key role. This may be a slow process; however, the directors can facilitate the process in the following ways (Antonisse, Cunningham, Hahn, and Harvey):

- Help set a positive tone and attitude for their faculty by promoting the value of library instruction
- Help standardize communication with faculty

- Help market agreed-upon expectations and learning outcomes

- Help communicate with faculty on behalf of librarians

- Offer opportunities to partner with librarians at campus conferences, committees, and so forth

Disciplinary distinctions between departments are also important, as there are differences in the research behavior of faculty in the social sciences, natural sciences, and humanities. They use information in varying ways and from a variety of resources; they use the library and view information literacy differently; and they may have a wide spectrum of opinion on what collaboration means. For example, the social science faculty often makes considerable use of the library, tapping into both print and online resources, statistical data sets, reference works, and government documents. The natural science faculty focuses on experimental work in the lab, which may leave them with little need to consult the library resources. Those who do, rely on online scholarly journal articles and data sets, with empirical research from the last five years being of primary importance. Humanities scholars, on the other hand, may not focus on currency to the same degree, favoring instead primary sources that include eyewitness accounts, journals, and documents from earlier time periods (Leckie, p. 202). Knowing the particular expectations and criteria of individual disciplines will enable librarians to personalize library–department interaction. It may also be important to listen closely to ways in which various disciplines use similar terms but assign distinctly different meanings to them, prime examples being "research" and "primary source." If a faculty member requires students to find primary source documents, it can be useful to ask the faculty member, "For the purposes of this assignment, how do you define a primary source?" It is also helpful to be aware of different disciplinary preferences for footnotes, endnotes, or in-text citations because these reflect distinct disciplinary approaches.

I strongly recommend that librarians developing a relationship with a department take the initiative to establish some common ground. Ideally, mentors within the library will pave the way based on previous relationships with these departments. It is not unusual for new academic librarians to be surprised at their own timidity in their initial meeting with individual tenured faculty or with the department as a whole, so it may be helpful to collaborate with an experienced colleague in the library. For example, the collections librarian or library instruction coordinator might offer support and statistics concerning library acquisitions, circulation, or instructional models (classes, labs, online Web pages, etc.) that have been successful with other departments.

Topics you might discuss in a meeting with a department could include these:

- Background of the new library liaison

- Introduction to new library resources and programs, such as new databases, updated interfaces on familiar databases, electronic interlibrary loan, e-reserve options, and course-specific Web-based research guides

- Faculty questions and concerns about library resources with specific reference to collection development

- Faculty members' observations on areas of possible acquisitions and/or weeding

- Past practice of handling acquisitions requests; questions and/or clarification of process

- Faculty's view of library instruction. Past history of successful relationships. Options for course-integrated library instruction. Usefulness of generic information literacy workshops, if a practice in the library

- Research competencies the department members would like their student majors to have upon graduation

- Courses that incorporate these competencies

- Assignments that traditionally tap library resources

- Ways in which additional library assistance might be beneficial

- Specialized research of faculty members in the department

- Other services the library can offer

Faculty frequently are not used to personalized service, which means that a proactive, outreach program is both needed and beneficial. Susan Barnes Whyte suggests the following questions:

- What do you want your students to know about library research and using the Web?

- Are you generally satisfied with their research?

- What do you think students in your department need to know in terms of library research when they graduate?

- What is your perception of students' frustrations and/or satisfaction with the library?

- How do you do library research?

- What are your frustrations and/or satisfactions with our library?

Kathy DeMey in her LOEX 2004 presentation on "How Do You Teach? Conversations & Collaborations" outlined the questions she asked faculty about research literacy:

- What level of research is expected of students in your upper-level courses? In the basic core courses?

- What kinds of research assignments do you give? How could we librarians help to support those assignments better?

- What goes on in the research methods courses in your discipline, if you have such courses?

For questions the librarians at the University of Maryland ask faculty, see www.lib.umd.edu/UES/communication.html.

In addition to a meeting with the department as a whole, hands-on department-specific workshops for faculty have also been popular. Faculty members may need to upgrade their own information literacy skills, even if one does not label it that way. Having worked in a very focused area of scholarly research, they may not be familiar with the wider range of resources linked to their discipline and perhaps with interdisciplinary resources such as *WorldCat*, full-text newspapers, government documents, datasets, scholarly Web sites, and so forth. Moreover, aggregators are frequently changing (1) their interfaces (2) the database of journals indexed, and (3) advanced searching techniques, all of which have a direct impact on faculty and student research. Many faculty are unaware of the complexity of resources that students face and find it quite eye opening to view library research from this perspective. Discovering that students do not have experience with the scholarly communication process often changes teaching faculty's views about working with librarians on student research projects. In addition, of course, the issues of plagiarism, Web site evaluation, copyright, and the types of assignments that may take account of these are of particular interest. All of these topics are part of librarians' areas of expertise. Let this be known!

Librarians must keep a flexible approach, matching their departmental contact with the faculty's pedagogy and previous practice. If there has been little collaboration with a department in the past, it may be helpful to establish a relationship with individual faculty members first (Raspa and Ward, p. 2). If the department has someone who handles dissemination of *Choice* cards, this person might be a good contact for scheduling an initial meeting as well as arranging to consult with the rest of the department. Having a library advocate within a department is an indispensable resource. Try to develop such a relationship, for nothing is as effective as having an advocate say to colleagues in the same department, "I just had a great brainstorming session with our liaison librarian about my course's assignments and resources." A librarian's goal is to be a peer with an area of specialization that complements that of teaching faculty.

With this in mind, be sure to contact new faculty members early in the semester. Give them a tour of the library; discover their particular area of scholarly research; discuss the courses they may be teaching; explore whether their students will be doing research that involves library resources; and offer your services in terms of collection development, acquisitions, instruction, and/or creation of course-specific resources guides and tutorials. The way librarians collaborate with faculty is usually contingent upon the way the faculty design their courses. The key is to learn about this and then let them know about the range of library resources and the areas of expertise that you can provide.

The success of the Earlham model of library instruction as well as a number of other studies has shown that course-related/integrated library instruction is considerably more effective than generic information literacy modules. The Mellon Foundation has played a significant role, through grant-funded projects, in promoting this approach. A number of liberal arts colleges (for example, Carleton and Oberlin) have received grants supporting the integration of information literacy into various curricula through partnerships between departments, libraries, and instructional technology centers. The Mellon Foundation has also funded information literacy initiatives by regional consortia such as the Associated Colleges of the Midwest (ACM), the Ohio Five, and the Midwest Instructional Technology Center (MITC), which is a joint enterprise of the ACM and the GLCA. If your institution has the staff and resources to provide course-related or integrated library instruction, take advantage of this. There are a number of approaches one might take to initiate such instruction:

- Contact faculty in the liaison departments early in the semester to determine which courses will have research projects so that classes may be scheduled.

- Obtain a copy of the research assignment and perhaps the class syllabus.

- Take the opportunity to meet with the course teacher to hear about the course goals and objectives, and to share areas of library expertise that would complement these.

- Discover if the faculty member has set a date for the students to hand in their topics, research questions, or hypotheses, and suggest that these be passed on to the librarian. Why? So, that the course-related library instruction can focus on the students' topics.

- Explore the possibility of joining the class e-mail list. This will put you in the loop with topic submission and ongoing research questions that students submit.

- Consider a brief pre-class survey on the resources with which students have had previous experience and/or search skills.

- Be willing to offer, if you have the time, to review student bibliographies for consistency in style format, as well as the inclusion of mutually agreed upon (with the professor) types of resources. This will give you and research instruction additional credibility. Grades count in the eyes of students and faculty.

- If possible, assess with the faculty member the use of library resources by students in their final research. This gives library instruction greater weight and ascertains the effectiveness of library instruction.

Establishing the groundwork for successful library–faculty partnerships takes time. Faculty may be protective of their turf. Sensing that there is already too little time allotted to teach the essential knowledge of their subject area, they may be chary of adding nondisciplinary material (for example, information literacy) and sharing this time with a colleague. If issues of pedagogy, as opposed to course content, are not a priority, librarians' desire to imbue their students with proficiency in the research process may play a secondary role to the faculty's desire to pass on disciplinary knowledge. Successful partnerships may run the gamut ranging from one-shot instruction classes to a close partnership in designing assignments and assessment tools.

Librarians need to be patient and flexible in matching their areas of expertise with teaching faculty's interests and expectations, course content, and student needs (Hutchins, Fister, and MacPherson, p. 3). In addition to liaison programs, there are other opportunities for collaborating with faculty. For example, on a number of campuses First Year Seminars and Learning Communities fully integrate library research modules into the curriculum. With other institutions, online course-specific research guides and highly developed Web-based tutorials play an important role in both e-learning on campus and distance learning off-campus. Prime examples of course specific research guides may be found on the Web page of the St. Olaf College Libraries (www.stolaf.edu/library), along with guides for endnote and citation styles, and links to information literacy sites. Examples of information literacy tutorials include TILT (University of Texas) at tilt.lib.utsystem.edu, RIO (University of Arizona) at www.library.arizona.edu/rio, CORE (Purdue) at core.lib.purdue.edu, and Information Literacy Tutorial (Minneapolis Community and Technical College) at www.mctc.mnscu.edu/Library/tutorials/infolit. Links to additional online teaching resources may be found through PRIMO, the online database of "Peer Reviewed Instructional Materials Online" provided by ACRL's IS Committee on Emerging Technologies in Instruction at cooley.colgate.edu/dbs/acrlprimo/showrec.html.

Sometimes librarians are included in discussion boards and chat rooms with both individual students and classes. Judging teaching and learning solely through students' in-class experience fails to account for the rapid changes in teaching and pedagogy both on and off campus. Increasingly, Teaching and Learning Centers address such changes and provide academic librarians with additional opportunities to work with faculty. Show up at discussions or participate in panels on topics such as the needs of today's students, the first year experience, teaching and learning styles, assessment, uses of instructional technology, information literacy, and distance learning.

Other areas that open the door to successful relationships with faculty include membership on committees and newly organized task forces, attendance at faculty meetings, and involvement in unions where they exist. In particular, library representation on a curriculum committee plays a key role in supporting current courses, anticipating future courses, and participating in faculty conversations as a peer. Being increasingly visible and contributing to current campus initiatives supports successful working relationships with faculty without adding new programs. If academic librarians can publicly demonstrate (i.e., market) their professional expertise, teaching faculty will see it as complementing both teaching and scholarly research (Grassian, p. 22). Such a partnership crosses that seeming cultural divide between teaching faculty and academic librarians.

Conclusion

Context is everything, and being able to read the culture of your institution and its departments is fundamental to your success as an academic librarian. Higher education may seem like a foreign country, especially if you have not received mentoring through the initial culture shock. Although the MLS degree might serve as a passport for getting on campus, understanding the assumptions, practices, and expectations of the inhabitants is not easy. As previously discussed, there may be significant power differentials between librarians and teaching faculty, which are felt but not acknowledged. However, academic librarians are indispensable to the success of our college students, so the bottom line is to affirm that teaching faculty and librarians share the same goals. Promoting our areas of expertise as complementary to that of classroom teachers and collaborating with them will enhance faculty teaching and support student learning. Forming successful library–faculty partnerships is at the heart of strong academic programs in higher education. It is also incredibly rewarding.

Works Cited

Antonisse, Peggy, Maggie Cunningham, Trudi Bellardo Hahn, and Diane Harvey. "Strategies for Partnering with Faculty to Teach Information Literacy." Presentation at *Library Instruction: Restating the Need, Refocusing the Response, LOEX 2004 Conference*, (Detroit, MI: May 8, 2004).

Barr, Robert B., and John Tagg. "From Teaching to Learning: A New Paradigm for Undergraduate Education." *Change*, 27.6 (1995): 12–25.

Breivik, Patricia S. "Making the Most of Libraries in the Search for Academic Excellence." *Change*, 19.4 (1987): 46.

Christiansen, Lars, Mindy Stombler, and Lyn Thaxton. "A Report on Librarian-Faculty Relations from a Sociological Perspective." *Journal of Academic Librarianship*, 30.2 (2004): 116–121.

Grassian, Esther. "Do They Really Do That?" *Change*, 36.3 (2004): 22–27.

Hardesty, Larry. "Faculty Culture and Bibliographic Instruction: An Exploratory Analysis." *Library Trends*, 44 (1995): 339–367.

Haynes, Evelyn B. "Librarian–Faculty Partnerships in Instruction." *Advances in Librarianship*, 20 (1996): 191–220.

Hill, Janet Swan. "Wearing Our Own Clothes: Librarians as Faculty." *Journal of Academic Librarianship*, 20.2 (1994): 72–73.

Hutchins, Elizabeth O. "Teaching as a Live Encounter: Sharing Our Authentic Self Invites Student Learning." *Reflective Teaching: A Bridge to Learning*, ed. Deb Biggs Thomas (Ann Arbor, MI: Pierian Press, 2004): 105.

Hutchins, Elizabeth O., Barbara Fister, and Kris (Huber) MacPherson. "Changing Landscapes, Enduring Values: Making the Transition from Bibliographic Instruction to Information Literacy." *Journal of Library Administration*, 36.1/2 (2002): 3–19.

Iannuzzi, Patricia. "Faculty Development and Information Literacy: Establishing Campus Partnerships." *Reference Services Review*, 26.3/4 (1998): 97–102.

Kreitz, Patricia A. "Librarians as Knowledge Builders: Strategic Partnering for Service and Advocacy." *College and Research Libraries News*, 65.1 (2004): 8–10, 15.

Leckie, Gloria. "Desperately Seeking Citations: Uncovering Faculty Assumptions about the Undergraduate Research Process," *Journal of Academic Librarianship*, 22.3 (1996): 202, 205.

Leckie, Gloria, and Anne Fullerton. "The Roles of Academic Librarians in Fostering a Pedagogy for Information Literacy." ACRL Ninth National Conference (April 8–11, 1999), ACRL. Available 24 June 2004: http://www.ala.org/ala/acrl/acrlevents/leckie99.pdf

Mitchell, W. Bede, and Bruce Morton. "On Becoming Faculty Librarians: Acculturation Problems and Remedies." *College & Research Libraries*, 53.5 (1992): 10, 379–392.

Rader, Hannelore B. "Building Faculty–Librarian Partnerships to Prepare Students for Information Fluency: The Time for Expertise Is Now." *College and Research Libraries News*, 65.2 (2004): 74–76, 80, 83, 90.

Raspa, Dick, and Dane Ward. "Listening for Collaboration: Faculty and Librarians Working Together." in *The Collaborative Imperative*, ed. Dick Raspa and Dane Ward (Chicago: Association of College and Research Libraries, 2000): 1–18.

Snavely, Loanne, and Natasha Cooper. "Competing Agendas in Higher Education: Finding a Place for Information Literacy." *Reference & User Services Quarterly*, 37.1 (1997): 53–62.

Whyte, Susan Barnes. "Conversations Betwixt and Between: Guiding Principles." *Reference Services Review*, 30.4 (2002): 269–276.

Building the Profession—Research, Creative Activities, and Publication by Academic Librarians

Joan Beam and Cathy Cranston

"If we knew what we were doing it wouldn't be research."
—Albert Einstein (1879–1955)

Academic librarians have a broad diversity of job descriptions and bear a variety of titles. Some may hold full faculty status with all the privileges and requirements of the research and teaching faculty, while others may be called academic faculty, administrative professionals, or classified staff. Not all academic institutions require publishing by their librarians, especially those that do not grant full faculty status. Yet, academic librarians frequently require publication or creative activities of themselves, with or without the motivational pressure of looming tenure or promotion. They find the inspiration and incentive to publish from personal inner resources. Academic librarians may publish or perform creative activities to fulfill an internal desire to share their knowledge or expertise in their area of librarianship. They may present at conferences and publish in proceedings to raise their profiles within their profession, or to enhance their reputations in order to progress onto higher career goals they have set for themselves. Some academic librarians may publish or create alternative methods of communication via Web sites and blogs in order to add to the body of knowledge in another subject area outside of librarianship. Perhaps they do so because they are a liaison to an academic department, or because they have a degree in another field.

"Publish or perish" is a phrase usually assigned to the tenure and promotion process, but to many academic librarians the need to publish
is to avoid a perishing of their own professional pride.

Academic librarians, like their counterparts in special, school, and
public libraries, have full-time positions that tend to be locked into
the structured workweek, without a great deal of free or discretionary
time. Most university and college librarians work twelve-month contracts, unlike their teaching faculty colleagues. Some librarians are
tied to stacks of original cataloging or public-service desk schedules
and often work eight-hour days that include evening or weekend
shifts, yet somehow they manage to include research, creative activities, and publication in this time. How do they do it? Who in the field
of academic librarianship actually publishes and why do they do it?
What kinds of works are produced, and how often? What is the need
for publishing in library and information science, which some have
described as more of a practical trade than a profession? It is very true
that librarians are practitioners as well as professionals, but this leads
even more for the need to publish and share one's ideas.

Publication

It is a given that publication is a basic requirement in order to
maintain library science as a profession. Publication is necessary, not
merely to maintain faculty status for the profession or for an individual to achieve tenure or promotion, but to add to the body of knowledge that goes into creating our professional literature. Librarianship
has undergone tremendous changes in the last decade, redefining
our roles on campus and in the larger world. How can we communicate these changes and suggest successful methods to adapt to
changes without a body of professional literature? How can we contribute to the functioning of our academic institutions without producing various creative activities to build networks between
departments? How can we assist in our institutions' teaching mission
without contributing works that aid in bibliographic instruction and
basic information literacy of the student body? How can we improve
access to collections and information without sharing methods of
bibliographic control? Research, creative activities, presentations,
and publication are professional necessities for all academic librarians, regardless of job description, academic rank, or status.

In a review of the literature, Weller, Hurd, and Wiberley reported that academic librarians at schools with Ph.D. programs publish more often than librarians at master's-level institutions. The most prolific authors came from libraries at Research I or ARL libraries with holdings surpassing one million volumes. Regardless of where the academic librarian was employed, the authors' review of the literature also indicated that the publication patterns of academic librarians included a steady increase in the number of peer-reviewed articles produced over the years 1993 to 1997. Sources indicate that academic librarians did most of their publishing in the realm of library literature. The majority of the articles were single authored, 55 percent, while 45 percent had two or more authors, although only 10 percent of the published articles had three or more. Weller, Hurd, and Wiberley also found that in the peer-reviewed core list of library science journals that they examined in their study, almost 80 percent of the academic librarians who published were single or co-author on only one publication in the five-year time period studied. In another article, Kathleen E. Joswick analyzed publication by Illinois librarians and discovered that more women academic librarians are publishing than in the past, when male librarians, despite lower numbers within the profession, tended to publish more articles. She also found that women tend to favor collaborative authorship, and that overall during the period of study, 1995–1999, the vast majority of authors only published one article. Again, large institutions produced more librarian authors than smaller ones. Most articles published by academic librarians appeared in journals within the field of library science, rather than outside the field. Thus we see that larger institutions produce more authors of peer reviewed articles than smaller ones, that women are increasing their productivity in the publishing world to reflect their numbers within the profession, but that essentially most academic librarians produce about one article over a given time period of five years and tend to publish in library-related journals. Of course, both of these studies limited their analysis strictly to peer-reviewed articles in journals, which leaves out a vast realm of alternative venues for publication.

Academic librarians tend to publish more than librarians working in other types of libraries regardless of the size of their institution or the definition of their position. In spite of busy and rigid work schedules, an academic librarian frequently manages to write at least one solo-author, peer-reviewed journal article. What are their reasons for going to the effort to produce publications and creative activities? Is it in response to requirements for tenure? Mitchell and Reichel surveyed research, doctoral, and master's degree institutions and found of the responding 690 institutions, 54.2 percent had tenure track librarians, and of these 60.9 percent required publication and 34.6 percent strongly encouraged it. The institutions also reported that 92.2 percent of their librarians who underwent tenure review during the three-year study period achieved it. Clearly, not only was publication strongly required, but these librarians were meeting the requirement. We can assume that the pressure to publish to achieve tenure encourages librarians to write for publication. However, librarians who are not tenure track also publish for other reasons. Montanelli and Stenstrom found that librarians will publish not only for advancement in rank, but also to achieve personal recognition and to improve their relationships with the teaching faculty on campus, and that publishing tends to correlate with advancement to leadership positions and greater success within the profession.

If you are a new member of the profession, and recently hired by an academic institution, with or without tenure and promotion requirements, but with a desire to publish, how do you get started? We all have experience writing papers, perhaps even full theses, depending on our previous academic experience. Publication is merely the next step, taking your written work and getting it into the professional literature. In order to avoid reluctance, fear, or intimidation, start right away. Do not wait until you feel completely settled in your new job because it is too easy to allow that excuse to last for years. Start small if you need to boost your professional confidence. Most states have a library association with some form of newsletter or magazine. These state publications are always looking for work to publish, and encourage new authors. They may not be peer-reviewed, but they are a forum for your ideas. Book reviews are another way to get into print; look for journals that are seeking reviewers. If you are a subject specialist in another academic field, offer to review books for journals in that field, after you have made clear exactly what your special credentials are in that area. Library conferences at the state or regional level actively seek presenters for their annual meetings, and these presentations can quickly lead to an article. Examine your daily activities, find a unique approach to a problem or issue you deal with every day, present it at a conference, write it up, and send it to a journal that publishes articles in your area.

All components of the academic library have their representative journal whether it is library administration, bibliographic control, creation of metadata, information literacy and instruction, or reference. You can easily identify where your article or idea might be well received by reading the professional literature and acquainting yourself with the individual journal titles, their content, and their intended audiences.

Getting Started

Do you find it difficult to arrive at a publishable concept, or are you afraid your idea has already been thoroughly discussed in the literature? Keep up with the professional literature, not only to see what has been written, or what problems have been addressed already, but also to discover where the gaps still exist. If an idea has been discussed in one arena, see if you can offer an alternative approach from another perspective. By scanning a variety of library publications, you can determine the content, style, depth, focus, and intended audience of each publication. Weller, Hurd, and Wiberley include in their article a list of over thirty core-refereed journals in librarianship published in the U. S. and Canada. They even note the titles in which more than 33 percent of the authors are academic librarians. You can determine which publication would most be interested in your concept by examining their recent issues' contents. With our limited free time at work, scanning publications' tables of contents may suffice until you find the articles that appeal to your special interests. If you are at an institution with a limited number of subscriptions, sign up for a table of contents service through a database vendor, such as *ingenta*. Perhaps your unique situation is new to the library world and no one has presented the problem at all, much less proposed a solution. If you find that true, you have an opportunity to contribute to the professional literature by offering practical advice. Be sure to write up your idea in a context applicable across a broad spectrum of libraries so that others may incorporate your ideas into their own library situation. The purpose of sharing one's expertise or experience is to assist others in their own institution's framework, not just to describe how you handled the problem.

Once you have determined your audience, found the publication you feel will be the best venue to present your ideas, prepared a well-researched and well-written article, and sent it off to the publication's editorial board, you must wait for a decision. Hopefully the decision will come quickly that your article has been accepted and will appear in an upcoming issue. Nevertheless, sometimes the article is returned, rejected for no reason that you are able to perceive. Take some comfort in knowing that you are not alone if this happens. It is distressing to spend hours, weeks, or even months on an article only to have it returned to you with polite words of rejection, but it happens to everyone. Learn from the experience just what went wrong. Had you prepared the journal to expect your article? Did you contact the editors in advance, letting them know about your idea and asking if they were interested in publishing something on the topic? Did you read recent issues of the journal to determine the style used by previous authors for depth of scholarship needed? Did you follow the format the journal requires for a literature review, methods of your survey or research, summary of your results, conclusion, and need for further research if any? Was there a recent flurry of publication in other journals on your topic that no one could have predicted? Did your selected journal undergo a recent change of administration, or focus, or did the editor leave, replaced by someone less interested in your topic? Not all rejection is your responsibility. Sometimes forces beyond our control cause journals to shift their focus or audience, change their editorial staff, or redefine their mission. Be sure to write your article well and to present your theme or idea clearly. Always have another colleague whose writing skills and honesty you trust review your article before you send it off. Others can see errors that we ourselves are blind to because we are too close to the subject. Identify another journal that might be interested in your idea, then send off your manuscript again to another journal and hope this time it is well received. If it is rejected, try another journal. You may not have correctly identified the proper audience initially, and it takes some experience to get it right.

If you were solicited by a journal to write an article, or sent in an unsolicited manuscript that appeals to the journal's editors, but have it returned for corrections, further research, or editing, take this in a positive manner. This is an opportunity to improve your writing style, your research methods, or the quality of your data. Work quickly to submit the corrected manuscript because often an editor already has it scheduled as part of an upcoming issue. Sometimes reviewers will send back conflicting suggestions for improvements. Try to determine the overall intention of their suggestions as you perform the corrections, rather than answering specific criticisms. Look at the larger picture and respond to that when submitting your revised manuscript.

Writing a Book

Some academic librarians decide at a point in their career that they are ready for book publishing. This is not advised for the newly hired untenured librarian expected to achieve full faculty status with tenure and promotion within five or six years. Books are a major undertaking, involving far more time and effort than one might anticipate. Always float your idea to publishers before beginning. Write to a series editor if you feel you can contribute another volume in the same theme. Send in a short proposal to the editors of a publishing house that offers titles in your area of interest. Be prepared to submit a writing sample, an outline, and reasons why your book would be a contribution to scholarship. Explain how it would be unique, what it would offer that no other book has, or perhaps how it would deal with a common problem with a unique perspective, or updated research. Remember that book publishers need to sell their products and make a profit, and your concept must have a necessary amount of salability for a publisher to be interested. It is up to you to convince the editors and publishers that your book concept is worth not only your investment of time but also their investment of resources. An excellent step-by-step guide to the process of book publishing can be found in Priscilla K. Shontz's book *Jump Start Your Career in Library and Information Science*. She includes guidelines for picking your publisher and walks you through the steps of generating ideas, choosing a co-author, submitting a proposal, negotiating the contract, writing the book, editing it, and finally submitting the completed manuscript. She cautions that book publishing is time consuming, and there can be a gap between submission of the final manuscript and the actual production of the monograph. Take this as a reminder that librarians with deadlines for accomplishing the requirements for tenure and promotion within a given time frame should be sure to start early on any book they plan to include in their tenure dossier. An as-yet-unpublished book might look fine after successfully publishing several journal articles in peer-reviewed journals because it shows you are continuing in your creative efforts. However, depending upon your institution, an unpublished monograph may not satisfy the requirements for tenure if the work is your only publication effort in your tenure package, or if your only other publications are book reviews or other early efforts at publication. Try to start a book early enough in your tenure process to guarantee publication by the time you submit your publication record to the tenure committee.

You should not be overwhelmed by all this advice on publishing if you remember to start small. It took years to become an academic librarian, and it will take time to become a published author. You will make mistakes, your efforts might not be initially rewarded or recognized, but if you persevere, you will ultimately succeed. Consider collaboration with an experienced author to get started. Having a mentor at your institution or in your area of expertise is a great way to start on your publishing path. They have the experience to help direct your efforts most profitably and successfully for your career.

As Rachel Singer Gordon states at the outset of *The Librarian's Guide to Writing for Publication*, "Always keep in mind that you are qualified to write for the profession merely by being part of the profession." For some librarians getting started is the most difficult step in the whole process of publishing. Highly motivated library school students who publish before they are out of school will certainly have a competitive edge when trying to land their first professional appointment. Collaboration with an experienced faculty member or taking on a small initial project is the likeliest route to publication during the nascent librarian years. Consider colleagues from library school or other junior faculty as writing partners as well.

A work environment that includes generous established librarians willing to offer a co-authoring opportunity to a new librarian, or support from the library administration in the form of time and professional development funds, can make all the difference. When interviewing for positions, a perceptive candidate will try to gauge these factors by talking with longtime and newer librarians as well as members of the tenure/promotions committee. If publication is required for tenure and promotion, these conversations might reveal "unofficial standards," such as the necessity of having a solo article or first authorship, or consideration of non-peer-reviewed publications.

It is a good idea to have a preliminary research agenda mapped out before interviewing in order to address the inevitable question regarding research interests. Research agendas may change once fully engaged in the profession, but it shows foresight to be prepared to speak about publishing interests. Once offered a position, it is essential to know the expectations in order to make an informed decision. Are work hours available for writing? What percentage of your time is expected to be used for publishing? If you work in a tenure-granting library, be sure to review and understand the promotion and tenure guidelines before accepting a position. Take into account not only the library policies, but also the university policies that will come into play, especially regarding copyright ownership of creative works. These policies vary from one institution to the next, and the nuances can be critical. Request policy documents once you have an interview set up so that any questions can be addressed at the on-campus interview.

Once you have the job, the obvious starting point for your writing career is to share a unique and successful part of your work experience. Keep in mind that even projects that do not turn out as intended may yield information worthy of sharing with a broader audience. It is easy to track the progression of academic librarianship into the digital age because librarians have been writing about it as they have experienced it. Topics include new ways to offer traditional library services and descriptions of the hi-tech methods of managing today's libraries. Despite the new topics, the traditional mode of academic publication is still in place for the time being. Well-established journals and peer-reviewed publications are the safest route for publishing if tenure is an issue, but many online and open-access publications are beginning to become an established part of the literature. Perhaps a few years from now librarians will feel even more comfortable in these publishing venues and set an example for faculty in other disciplines. Depending on institutional policies, some libraries may rank journals and assign more weight to articles published in research-based journals. Find out early how high you should be aiming when designing your research projects and approaching publishers. As noted by Bradigan and Mularski, librarians on the tenure track often do not have the information they need about specific criteria used in the evaluation of their work. Be proactive and seek out this information.

Sending a completed article directly to a journal without some initial information gathering can be risky. Check to make sure there is a general interest in the field in order to convince the editor of your idea's viability. Do not always take the opinion of one editor as the final word. You have the option to shop your idea to other publications before giving up. Sometimes an editor will attempt to turn your article into something it is not in order to get it to conform to the theme of a topical issue. This may or may not be possible, depending on the subject, but ultimately the work needs to stand up to review by the broader audience of librarians. If your article receives special recognition by being chosen for a cover article or featured with full-text availability, this exposure can lead to name recognition, offers for future collaboration, and significant impact in the profession.

Librarians' Experiences

Three untenured library faculty members at Colorado State University were interviewed regarding the publication part of their professional responsibilities. Each is within a year of going up for tenure and has had success with publishing. Some common themes arose from these interviews. The environment at Colorado State University has spurred these librarians to author as many as 17 refereed articles between them, as well as many others in nonrefereed publications. Each of the librarians made an early start with their publishing activities; one had a short article based on a conference review in print only six months after starting a professional job. The new job duties of this generation of librarians reveal themselves in the content of the articles, which included topics such as Web tools for collection development, PHP programming for dynamic content, and Web-based instruction. One of the librarians passed on this sage advice received from a mentor, "Every time you do something, think of the publishing possibilities." So far, each new librarian has chosen well-established journals in which to publish. Although all were aware of open-access journals in their field, they did not feel that it was worth the risk to publish in these lesser-known journals. However, publishing in peer-reviewed journals outside of the library literature was certainly an option, as one librarian noted, "An old idea in librarianship might be a brand new idea to educators." Even though it may exceed the minimum requirement for tenure, the goal of trying to get something in print in a refereed journal each year will stand a junior librarian in good stead. As rejection is always a potential outcome, and sometimes beyond your control, it is prudent to have a backup writing project in the works. Do not delay publishing aims, as the timeframe for getting through the publication cycle can put a kink in the tenure or promotion calendar if left until the last minute. Each of the librarians emphasized this point: "Start early, and don't rest on your laurels after your first success."

It is not necessary that the tenure requirement for research and creative activity be a part of the working environment in order to stimulate publication by librarians. Many academic librarians often discover a real sense of personal satisfaction from translating their ideas into print. Contributing to the literature for the sake of saving other librarians time, energy, and duplication of effort is at the heart of our work ethic. One does not need years of experience to find a niche of librarianship that can use some fresh analysis resulting in surprising insight. Have the self-confidence to get started, and you will find that the process is much more accessible than you might have thought. Research and publication builds on the interests and skills that brought you to the profession to begin with: the desire to seek out information and share it with our clientele. Instead of sharing information over a reference desk or in a classroom, you are sharing it in a presentation at a conference, over a Web site, or in a book chapter or journal article. Remember that your creative activities and publication efforts are contributing to the professional body of literature. Keeping librarianship relevant is important to the larger world of scholarship and to the success of faculty research in all disciplines. You can make an important contribution to the goals of the entire academic community in educating new generations of students.

Works Cited

Bradigan, Pamela S., and Carol A. Mularski. "Evaluation of Academic Librarians' Publications for Tenure and Initial Promotion." *The Journal of Academic Librarianship*, 22.5 (1996): 360–365.

Gordon, Rachel Singer. *The Librarian's Guide to Writing for Publication.* Lanham, MD: Scarecrow Press, 2004.

Haas, Leslie, Suzanne Milton, and Aimee Quinn. "Surviving the Publishing Process: A Beginner's Guide." *RQ*, 36.2 (1996): 230–237.

Joswick, Kathleen E. "Article Publication Patterns of Academic Librarians: An Illinois Case Study." *College and Research Libraries,* 60.4 (1999): 340–349.

Labaree, Robert V. "Tips for Getting Published in Scholarly Journals: Strategies for Academic Librarians." *College and Research Library News,* 65.3 (2004): 137–139.

Mitchell, W. Bede, and Mary Reichel. "Publish or Perish: A Dilemma for Academic Librarians?" *College and Research Libraries,* 60.3 (1999): 232–43.

Montanelli, Dale S. and Patricia F. Stenstrom. "The Benefits of Research for Academic Librarians and the Institutions They Serve." *College and Research Libraries,* 47 (1986): 482–85

Shontz, Priscilla K. *Jump Start Your Career in Library and Information Science.* Lanham, MD: Scarecrow Press, 2002.

Weller, Ann G., Julie M. Hurd, and Stephen E. Wiberley Jr. "Publication Patterns of U.S. Academic Librarians from 1993 to 1997." *College and Research Libraries,* 60.4 (1999): 352–362.

CHAPTER 4

Time Served Is Time Well Spent— Making the Most of Your Service Commitments

Michelle Mach

"A university should be a place of light, of liberty, and of learning."
—Benjamin Disraeli, Earl of Beaconsfield
(1804–1881)

What is service? Isn't it obvious? Actually, no. When I polled the COLLIB-L and NMRT-L listservs in the spring of 2004 about the service activities of academic librarians, more than one librarian asked for clarification. There are several reasons for this confusion. First, librarianship is a service-oriented profession. Even librarians who do not work directly with the public, such as catalogers, have user-focused goals. In a sense, everything you do in your library job *is* service. However, most positions that require service define it as outreach or committee activities that are "above and beyond" your normal duties. Second, every library, and probably every librarian, defines service differently. Some expect service in all categories (library, university, professional, and community), while others do not. Some limit service to committee work, whereas others employ a broader definition. As a new academic librarian, one of your first priorities should be to figure out how *your* institution defines service. Finally, research and scholarly/creative activities capture substantially more attention in articles, books, and conference programs than service. This focus probably stems from stories anxious tenure track faculty hear about denial of tenure for research-related problems, never for service. New librarians may receive ongoing support and guidance

43

for research projects, but they may simply be told to do "something" for service. This chapter will discuss the reasons for participating in service, the many types and levels of service available, how to select appropriate activities, and how to present your achievements for evaluation.

Why Do Service?

Why do librarians participate in service activities? The cynic might say, "Because it's required." It is true—for many librarian positions on college and university campuses, it *is* a job requirement. Even though this may be the initial reason some librarians get involved, it is not usually the reason they continue. Some common reasons for participating in service are learning about others, having a positive impact on someone's life, sharing expertise and ideas, developing new skills or deepening existing ones, networking and meeting new people, becoming part of a community, raising the visibility/respect of the library, and having fun.

In addition, specific service activities may reap specific benefits. Priscilla K. Shontz notes, "Serving on search or selection committees allows you to see what your colleagues and supervisors notice in resumes. It allows you to see others' resumes, and allows you to learn for your own future job interviews" (Shontz, *Jump Start* ..., p. 63). Some activities affect your institution, not just yourself. Kathy A. Turner (Florida Institute of Technology) discovered that serving as Faculty Senate President "made a huge difference in how librarians are perceived on campus." Participation in service may also lead to opportunities in other areas. At a previous institution, Allison V. Level (Colorado State University) worked with science faculty from several departments on a regional science, engineering, and mathematics conference for middle school students. Several members of the conference-planning group later wrote a successful National Science Foundation (NSF) grant.

Types of Service Activities

Committee work is the foundation of much campus and professional service. In fact, some librarians may view "committee work" and "service" as interchangeable terms. Committees may be labeled as working groups, teams, task forces, boards, councils, or round tables, but their purpose is the same: to carry out a particular charge. Some are permanent groups with long-term goals, and others are ad hoc groups brought together for short-term tasks. Some may focus on discussing issues, while others work toward a specific output such as a conference program or scholarship award. Some groups may do both. Committees may be comprised of librarians, administrators, faculty, staff, students, or community members, with membership ranging from two or three members to more than twenty.

Campus Service

Campus service may include both library and university work, depending on your institution. (Some libraries view library committee work as part of your job, rather than as service.) Both library and campus service commonly includes faculty governance, awards/scholarships committees, and search committees.

Library service opportunities may also include standing committees, particularly for cross-department issues like the library catalog, the Web site, or even social activities. Short-term task forces often investigate and recommend new library policies, resources, or services. Libraries may offer noncommittee service, such as organizing a library book sale, designing a Web page, or assisting a patron focus group. All library service offers a way to meet librarians and staff, often from different units and with different levels of experience. Depending upon the committee appointment schedule, a short-term committee may provide the quickest way for new librarians to become involved. As a bonus, short-term committees often have a cutting-edge focus, providing excellent background for future presentations or research.

University or college committee opportunities may include thesis/dissertation, budgets, grievance resolution, curriculum, publications, information technology or campus computing, student life, or athletics. There is often a library committee at the university level, providing the library representative with an outsider's view of the library. University committees often require multi-year commitments and appointments may be highly competitive.

Although university committees can be intimidating, they do offer an excellent way to figure out who the major players are and how things work at your particular institution. How is a college class added to the catalog? What causes some students to go on academic probation? How much money does the athletic department bring in, anyway? How do teaching faculty *really* feel about the library? Being able to confidently answer such questions, even if only for yourself, will help you feel more at home at your institution.

One way to become actively involved in a campus committee is to offer your skills as a librarian. For example, you might offer to research a topic of interest to the committee, such as the effect of smaller class size on student performance. Melody Layton McMahon (Jon Carroll University) created a catalog of all the documents required for the North Central Accreditation process of the school and was available for assistance during the site visit. While this process "consumed my life for about three weeks," it gave her "a different understanding of why certain things happen and how different parts of the university work together."

In addition to formal committees, you might also consider working with a particular population on campus. These groups may include racial, ethnic, or religious groups; adult learners; Greek organizations; disabled students; athletes; first generation college students; student government; international students; or honor societies. Your role with such groups will likely be less structured than formal committee assignments, maximizing your creativity and flexibility. Offer these groups library tours, instruction sessions, Web site design, research assistance, or whatever your areas of strength will allow you to provide.

Michael J. McLane (Central New York Library Resources Council), an academic librarian and library administrator for more than thirty years, observes that "the most enjoyable [campus] activities often involved working with/for students in nonlibrary situations." Many academic librarians agree. An advisor for undecided students, Susan A. Smith (State University of West Georgia) finds that "most [students] just need a little coaching and encouragement." Jill A. Chai (Texas Tech University) works as a mentor in the Mentor Tech Program, a program designed to enhance the quality of the educational experiences of African American and Hispanic students. She states, "I was glad to take this opportunity to interact with people from different cultural backgrounds, and found it a rewarding experience to be a mentor to my Hispanic protégé. I often e-mail information and articles that I think might be of interest to my protégé, and she responded positively."

Other librarians offer talks on librarianship as part of career day sessions. Another possibility is to help the groups achieve their own goals, like raising funds or organizing a conference.

Sometimes the size of your institution affects the kinds of campus opportunities available. At Beacon College, a small liberal arts college for students with learning disabilities, Dianna J. Wade works with students individually, knowing each of the eighty-five full-time students by name. She states, "To see them learn and develop socially, emotionally, and intellectually over the time they are here makes for an emotional graduation each spring!" Ruth Connell (Valparaiso University) played basketball as part of a campus fundraising tournament and served midnight breakfast to students right before finals. Occasionally, events may not turn out as you expect. Matthew R. Marsteller (Carnegie Mellon University) describes his unfortunate experience as a library mascot in the Pittsburgh St. Patrick's Day Parade: "Some overzealous mother of two came running up to me and gave me a big hug in the hopes that I would swing over to their side of the parade route when I got to that point. Little did she know, when she gave me that big bear hug, the head of my costume shifted back and the steel ring that normally would rest on my shoulders smacked me right in the forehead—just great—a loopy Lion staggering the downtown streets of Pittsburgh!"

Professional Service

Library association work appeals to many librarians because it "provides opportunities to work on real issues. For all that you read in books and study in library school, it is not the same as working to solve an issue that impacts your library, position, or profession." As a new librarian, it is easiest to become involved in your state or regional library association. Some libraries encourage service in national library organizations such as the American Library Association (ALA), Special Libraries Association (SLA), REFORMA (National Association to Promote Library and Information Services to Latinos and the Spanish-Speaking) or the National American Serials Interest Group (NASIG). The Library HQ site (www.libraryhq.com/orgs.html) lists most major library organizations.

New librarians do get appointments on national committees. Joining the New Members Round Table (NMRT) of ALA is one path to national committee service. NMRT helps new librarians (those with fewer than ten years of ALA membership) gain committee and leadership experience. Serving as an ALA committee intern is another way to become involved. Trudi E. Jacobson served as an intern for a year on the Education for Bibliographic Instruction Committee. She was required to take and distribute the meeting minutes and found it was "an excellent way to fit in immediately, and to get to know more about the working of the organization." In addition to library organizations, subject specialists may also wish to join associations in their discipline, such as the Modern Languages Association or the Society for Range Management. Some associations, like the American Society for Engineering Education, have divisions or sections specifically related to libraries. Nonlibrary organizations not only present a good way to keep current on your discipline and its major issues but also provide a refreshing "outsider" point-of-view on library issues.

Some common professional service activities include editing journals or newsletters, developing bylaws and procedures, creating related resources (either online or in print), judging competitions, arranging conference programs or panels, and serving as a liaison to other organizations. Association committees typically focus on primary job types or functions, current library issues, specific user populations, or library type. There are committees for awards, publications, standards, budgets, planning, membership—the list is nearly endless. Large organizations such as ALA even have a "Committee on Committees"!

In addition to committee appointments, there are also volunteer positions, such as listserv administrators, Webmasters, or newsletter editors. A few volunteer positions offer a stipend, making it possible to attend conference meetings. Another option is to start your own professional group. Kathleen F. Cohen (University of North Florida) served as the charter president of the Northeast Library Information Network, a library consortium. This group started as a monthly lunch group to discuss shared issues and solve problems.

Community Service

Community service offers the most opportunity for noncommittee work. Some libraries require that community service use your professional skills. Activities might include volunteering at the public library, sitting on the school board, or working with a local historical society. Scott Walter (Washington State University) works as a rater for the required senior research paper for a local high school. This activity allows him to work with "high school teachers interested in research skills and help promote the WSU Libraries K–12 outreach activities." A recent library science graduate, Jeff Moser, read for the Louisiana Voices books on tape. He states, "[It was] very rewarding to me personally, because I know there aren't that many books available in this format—and free to the public." Those who define "community" very broadly might follow in the footsteps of Kara Malenfant (DePaul University). Kara volunteered to help establish and organize an elementary school library in South Africa through the World Library Partnership's "Inform the World Program." "One day after school, we had more than 60 children in the room—under the card catalog, on top of tables, anywhere they could find a spot—but it was completely silent. They were totally engrossed in their books. It was an amazing experience" ("Service is second ..." p. 3).

Decisions, Decisions

As a new librarian, you may be appointed or "volunteered" for activities that do not interest you. Some library administrators favor this "sink or swim" technique because it forces new librarians to immerse themselves immediately in the academic environment. Try to make the best of it; you might be pleasantly surprised. Shelly McCoy (University of Delaware) describes her first service experience as a United Way solicitor within the library: "I do not like to ask people for money, so I wasn't too happy with it, but the experience turned out fine—it taught me how to write e-mails to the staff of the whole library asking for money."

Eventually, you should initiate at least some of your own service activities. Think about what activities you enjoy or identify groups of people that you would like to work with. View any written policies at the library on service activities. Then talk to your supervisor, your mentor, the chair of the evaluation/review team, and your colleagues with varying levels of tenure at that library. Ask to see vitas or annual lists of activities, preferably from those who have experience levels similar to yours. (The vita of a senior academic librarian can be daunting!) It is best to ask, rather than assume. The last thing you want is to work hard all year and have those evaluating you say, "So what?"

Do not be alarmed if everyone offers different advice; it may be simply that a wide range of activities are acceptable. In your conversations, two perspectives will probably emerge. The first is that as a professional you should present a cohesive package. That is, your librarianship (your primary job), your research/creative activity, and your service should join to form a cohesive whole. For example, an art librarian might teach art research classes to students, buy books for the art collection, write an article on how art faculty uses electronic journals, and as service, put together a student art exhibit at the library. The second viewpoint advocates participation in any activity, regardless of how it relates to your other duties. Sometimes this perspective is found at small college libraries where specialization is a luxury. It is also a way to get started in your first job, or as a way to transition to a new one. "If you would like some budgeting experience, try to get on a committee that manages a budget for a program or project. ... If you want to gain supervisory experience, volunteer to chair a committee or run for an office. Diversify your skills by participating in activities you can't perform on your daily job." There is no reason that the two perspectives need to be exclusive; you can certainly tie most activities together with a common theme and occasionally branch out to develop new skills.

In addition to considering how service may (or may not) fit with your other duties, you will want to examine the time factor. In some positions, you may be required to devote a specific percentage of your time to service activities. Theoretically, a 10 percent allotment means that you should devote four hours (out of forty) each week toward service. The problem is that service is not always something you can evenly divide throughout the year. Community outreach, for example, may take place primarily during the summer, and university committees may only operate during the school year. Work on professional committees may be intense immediately before and after conferences, but somewhat lax during the rest of the year. Examine your regular workflow. Would certain times of the year be better to concentrate on service? Be aware that depending on when you start your job, you may not be able to immediately find committee work. For example, ALA generally appoints new committee members only once a year, immediately following the annual conference in June. Finally, consider the time required for *all* your service activities. Will you have enough time for your other duties? If not, learn to say no, nicely but firmly.

Questions to Ask about Service

Ask Yourself:

- What kinds of activities do I enjoy?
- What skills would I like to learn or expand?
- Whom will I meet as a result of this service activity?
- What benefits might result from this activity?
- What size group do I feel comfortable working in?
- What can I offer to the group? How will I fit in?
- What are the costs (in time, money, effort) associated with the service activity?
- How does this service activity relate to my current job? To my research interests?
- What are the organization's political leanings or mission? Do those mesh with my own?
- How does the time requirement mesh with my work schedule? My personal schedule?
- Will I be able to publish or present as a result of this activity?

Ask Your Supervisor, Mentor, or Colleagues:

- Is there financial support for service commitments (conference travel, for example)?
- What kind of service opportunities are the most highly valued at this institution? Is breadth or depth favored?
- How closely should service activities be tied to my other duties like librarianship or research?
- How are librarians selected for library and university committees?
- How is library committee work viewed?
- How is editing or writing service viewed? (Does it count as research or service?)
- How much service is required? How is this measured (percentage of time, number of activities)?

- What level (community, university, state, national) of service is expected? What combination of activities?
- Would it be possible to see a sample vita or activity summary listing service activities?
- What kinds of service activities are popular at this institution?
- What kinds of service activities would you recommend for a new librarian?
- How did you first get involved in service activities?
- What kinds of activities besides committee membership are acceptable?
- How often will my service activities be reviewed? Who will do the reviewing?
- What type and format or service documentation is expected?

Ask the Service Activity Coordinator:
- Will I be expected to attend in-person meetings at conferences? If so, how many times per year?
- How much work goes on in between meetings? Is this primarily done by individuals or teams?
- Is online or "virtual" service a possibility?
- What kinds of leadership opportunities are available?
- What skills are required or recommended?
- How easy is it to become involved? Is there a formal process in place?
- Does the committee have an "end product" (such as a conference program) or is it more of a discussion group?
- What is the time commitment (number of hours, time of year, short-term, or ongoing?

Getting Started

Once you have a handle on what counts as a service activity at your institution, view Web sites of organizations that interest you. Many post meeting minutes, lists of members, official missions or charges, past accomplishments, future planned activities, and other information. Subscribe to listservs that interest you; many of them post calls for volunteers. Let colleagues at your current library and elsewhere know that you are interested in service. Often librarians currently serving on a committee can make membership recommendations. Many organizations have online forms for committee volunteers. Expect to explain on the form why you are a good match for this particular committee, or to rank committees in order of preference.

If possible, attend committee meetings in person before you decide. At those meetings, introduce yourself to the chair, explain your interest in the committee and highlight any previous related experience. If an in-person meeting is not possible, send an e-mail message to the chair. If you are not invited to your first choice committee, do not despair. Some committees are very popular. Often committee membership depends upon a certain balance of type of library, geographical location, ethnicity, gender, or length of time in the profession.

Sometimes you may get a terrific leadership opportunity sooner than you expected. If you feel up to the challenge, it can have a very positive impact on your career. Paul O. Jenkins (College of Mount St. Joseph) describes one of his first service experiences: "I was chosen to serve on the campus Mediation and Resolution of Disputes Committee. A very complex case involving a faculty member and the administration came before us and after we could not find any faculty member who would agree to act as Chairperson of the Hearing Panel assigned to settle the case, I volunteered. I was in my second year at the College, fresh out of graduate school, and fairly naïve. The case was settled to the satisfaction of the faculty at large, and I gained a relatively high profile on campus due to the role I played."

Evaluation of Service Activities

Before your first tenure, merit, or annual evaluation, find out who will review your work (if the process is not a blind review), whether this is a standing group or one with rotating membership, and the written and unwritten criteria. Many review guidelines contain a sentence like this: It shall be the librarian's responsibility to provide evidence of successful service. At minimum, this "evidence" should include an updated vita or summary of activities. Spell out any acronyms on first usage, as people outside of your department, library, or university may review your materials. Indicate committees that you chaired or in which you held a leadership role, such as secretary. Merely listing your service activities, however, may not be enough to ensure a high rating. Put yourself in the reviewer's place. How do they know whether you just sat there, or whether you actually contributed? Describe your activities in some detail. Similarly, doing identical service activities each year will not necessarily guarantee an identical rating. As job experience grows, so do expectations. A librarian with ten years of experience may be expected to chair at least one committee, while a new librarian may not.

Talk to your mentor or supervisor about the format and content of expected documentation. One possibility includes writing a description of the service, including the importance or impact of the work, challenges, accomplishments, time commitment, and your specific role or contribution. You may be required to write a self-appraisal or a description of your service philosophy, that is, why did you get involved in these particular groups and activities? If these items are required, ask to see samples from previous years. Other suggestions

---

Possible Inclusions in Service Dossier

- Letters or e-mails of commendation/acknowledgment from the committee chair, or others affected by your service activities
- Honors/awards received (a photograph works well if you received a plaque or other nonpaper award)
- Copies of official committee publications, such as standard and guidelines, technical reports, or monographs
- Grant proposals or award letters
- Conference programs
- Outlines or copies of presentations or panel participation, including any handouts
- Newsletters or magazine articles describing service activity
- Annual committee reports
- Meeting minutes, especially those that document your active role
- Philosophy of service statement
- Description or summary of service activities
- Self-evaluation statement of service
- Photographs that show your active service role or scope of project

for items to include in your service dossier are listed in the sidebar. Think about how to highlight your contribution. A description of service that includes the number of applicants, amount of documentation reviewed, and a list of award winners is more effective than the simple statement "served on awards committee." A photo of you surrounded by hundreds of cans of food is more powerful than "organized food drive."

Conclusion

Try to get involved in service your first year as an academic librarian. Better yet, start as a library school student. Priscilla Shontz states, "I wish I had known about committee involvement when I was a student; it would have put me ahead of other new graduates by helping me make contacts and giving me a better feel for both the association and the profession as a whole" (Shontz, *Jump Start* ..., p. 89). Start small, adding activities that are more ambitious as you gain confidence. Look beyond the obvious, like university committees, to see what other opportunities are available. "I do suggest jumping in with enthusiasm and energy, volunteering in a group or groups that interest and excite you. Try what is offered and be willing to fall on your face." Even negative experiences with ineffective committee chairs or unclear charges offer valuable learning experiences. Shelly McCoy (University of Delaware) advises new librarians to "go with the flow" and recognize that even if you do not enjoy that particular activity "it does not have to last your whole tenure at the library." Be persistent and flexible in seeking out service opportunities. Once you are known as an active participant who accomplishes projects on time, you will be sought out for committee appointments. In many organizations, there is more work to do than people to do it. Remember that you *can* make a tremendous difference in many lives.

Notes

In April 2004, I asked members of the COLLIB-L (College Librarians) and NEWLIB-L (New Members Round Table) listservs to share their observations and experiences regarding service activities. All the quoted comments and advice, except the cited references, were taken directly from the e-mails I received. Thanks to everyone who generously offered their wisdom and guidance.

Works Cited

Hopkins, Alison. "Surviving ALA." *Info Career Trends*, 2.4 (2001). Available 12 March 2004: www.lisjobs.com/newsletter/archives/jul01ahopkins.html

Jacobson, Trudi E. "From Timid New Committee Member to Vice-Chair/Chair-Elect." *Info Career Trends*, 2.4 (2001). Available 12 March 2004: www.lisjobs.com/newsletter/archives/jul01tjacobson.html

Nims, Julia. "Sharing the Benefits of Membership." *Info Career Trends*, 2.4 (2001). Available 12 March 2004: www.lisjobs.com/newsletter/archives/jul01jnims.html

"Service Is Second Nature for Librarian/Volunteer." *Newsline (DePaul University)*, Spring 2002.

Shontz, Priscilla K. "Getting Involved: NMRT." *Info Career Trends*, 2.4 (2001). Available 12 March 2004: www.lisjobs.com/newsletter/archives/jul01pshontz.html

Shontz, Priscilla K. *Jump Start Your Career in Library and Information Science*. Lanham, MD: Scarecrow Press, 2002.

CHAPTER 5

Faculty Status, Promotion, and Tenure—What Are You Getting Into?

Gwen Meyer Gregory and Mary Beth Chambers

"Tenure is the worst of personnel systems save for all the others."

—Robert O'Neil (1934–)

As an academic librarian, you should know about faculty status, promotion, and tenure. Faculty at most colleges and universities are awarded tenure, meaning that they have a continuing employment contract and can only be terminated for certain specified reasons, usually things like criminal conviction, commission of sexual harassment, or demonstrated dereliction of duty. To earn tenure, they normally go through a multiyear process of in-depth evaluations. At the end of some specified time, usually six or seven years, they are required to apply for tenure, also sometimes known as continuing contract. If they are not awarded tenure, they must leave their jobs within a specified period. They are also eligible for promotion through the faculty ranks, from assistant to associate to full professor. Thus, this process is sometimes known as promotion and tenure. Librarians with faculty status have the same rights and responsibilities as teaching faculty and will be part of the promotion and tenure system at their institutions. You will be required to create a dossier of your professional career; for more on this see Chapter 10.

Throughout the twentieth century and up to the present time faculty status has been a hotly debated issue among academic librarians. As early as the 1940s, selected academic librarians enjoyed some form of faculty status. In the 1960s, many librarians had some if not all of the benefits of faculty. In 1971, the Association of College and Research Libraries (ACRL) first adopted its "Standards for Faculty Status of College and University Librarians," most recently revised in 2001. Some institutions give librarians academic status, which recognizes librarians as professional staff but does not confer the rights and privileges of faculty. ACRL also has "Guidelines for Academic Status for College and University Librarians," approved in 2002. According to a 1995 survey, about half of the academic librarians in the United States have faculty status. The full results of this survey, with results on many questions about the wide variety of statuses possible for academic librarians, and some samples of documentation on the library promotion and tenure process are included in the ACRL's CLIP Note #26, *Criteria for promotion and tenure for academic librarians.* ACRL's 1999 report, *Academic Library Trends and Statistics,* showed similar results.

There are many variations of faculty and academic status for librarians. You may be considered faculty and treated just like the teaching faculty. You may be eligible for promotion but not tenure, or vice versa. You may have the same rank system as faculty, or other ranks such as assistant, associate, and senior librarian. The key is to understand the system at your school and how to succeed as a participant. To abide by the campus' faculty policies, you need to know what they are. If the library also has its own promotion and tenure policies and procedures, you must understand and follow them as well.

As with any discipline, librarianship is based on theory, practice, and standards that are unique to the field. Librarianship is a service profession because librarians serve users. In the words of Janet Swan Hill, "The ethical basis and values of librarianship are derived from its inherent service orientation." Yet, it is also an applied field, because as Hill said, "Testing, experimentation, and application are native to librarianship." For purposes of reappointment, promotion, or tenure, it is common for academic librarians to be evaluated not only on the basis of their practice of librarianship, the parallel to the teaching focus for nonlibrarian faculty, but also on the basis of their contributions to scholarly research, publication or creative works, and on the level of their professional service activities.

Benefits

If you accept a faculty appointment at an academic institution, you will discover that it comes with special benefits and privileges. As a member of the faculty, you will be held to high standards of excellence and professionalism that will in turn earn you status and respect among members of the intellectual community as a whole. In addition, although it is not always the case, as a faculty librarian the potential exists for you to earn a higher salary as compared to other employees within your institutional setting. This is particularly true if you work at a college or university where librarians hold academic standing and where salaries and promotions are keyed to academic rank. As a faculty member, when you receive a promotion in rank, for example a promotion from assistant professor to associate professor, most likely you will be awarded a salary increase at the same time.

The obligations of faculty status may seem daunting at times, but they will challenge you to engage in professional activities that you might not otherwise attempt, particularly scholarly pursuits such as research and publication. While any librarian can engage in scholarship, as an academic librarian with faculty status, you will likely work in an environment specifically geared toward it. It is an environment where research and publication, although required, are encouraged and supported by your supervisor and by your peers. If you accept a tenure track position, you will assume the role of scholar librarian.

Scholarship is intellectual or creative work undertaken by academics working within a discipline for advancing the discipline. Scholars typically communicate through publications, such as journal articles and books, where their work is reviewed and validated by other scholars in the field. Scholarship is essential to the long-term viability of any discipline including the theory and practice of librarianship. Furthermore, as an academic librarian, you should have the protection of academic freedom as described by the American Association of University Professors' 1940 Statement of Principles on Academic Freedom and Tenure. Academic freedom protects you, as a faculty member, from disciplinary action or censorship based on your choice of research or teaching topics. It is a hallmark of the academic tenure process.

Traditionally scholarship has emphasized the research and publication process. However, in 1990 Ernest Boyer, then President of the Carnegie Foundation for the Advancement of Teaching, in his book

Scholarship Reconsidered: Priorities of the Professoriate, challenged scholars to accept a less restrictive view of scholarship, embracing four primary areas: "the scholarship of discovery," the traditional, investigative form of research for the advancement of knowledge; "the scholarship of integration," the creation of knowledge connections or the synthesizing of knowledge across disciplines; "the scholarship of application," the advancement of knowledge through the practice of a discipline; and "the scholarship of teaching," the process of educating and encouraging future scholars. Inspired by the Boyer model, the Association of College and Research Libraries in 1996 charged the Task Force on Institutional Priorities and Faculty Rewards to write a formal statement to define and describe scholarship for academic librarians. This became known as the Academic Librarianship and the Redefining Scholarship Project. The final report of the Task Force issued in 1998 formally extended the range of academic librarian activities that could be recognized as scholarly for purposes of tenure, promotion, or merit. If you are considering a position as a faculty librarian, familiarize yourself with the recommendations outlined in the 1998 ACRL Task Force report (available from the ACRL Web page at www.ala.org/acrl) so that you are aware of how scholarship is interpreted for the library profession. Before accepting a faculty librarian position at any institution, make sure that you understand what activities are expected of you as a scholar librarian.

Engaging in research and publication can be intrinsically rewarding for you as a librarian and scholar. Beyond just the pleasure of seeing your name in print, you will be gratified to know that you have contributed to the body of knowledge for your discipline. Furthermore, you will want to translate your research into acceptable program proposals for national library conferences such as those sponsored by the American Library Association or by regional or state library organizations. In this way, you extend your scholarly reach as you build your professional dossier.

As an academic librarian, you will engage in service activities in addition to librarianship and scholarship. This will give you even greater opportunities for professional development. Service work for librarians may cover a wide range of activities including service to the profession, the library, the institution, or the community. However, it is likely that much of your service work will involve service to the profession. For instance, you may be involved in planning, organizing, or conducting professional workshops for librarians. Alternatively, you may be involved in conference or program planning for regional, state, or national library groups or organizations. Perhaps you will serve on a committee that establishes standards or guidelines for the practice of librarianship such as those sponsored by the American Library Association. Service opportunities abound, but they will not always fall into your lap. You may have to seek them out. Also, as a new librarian on the job, you need to work closely with your supervisor to determine the appropriate time and the appropriate degree of committee or service involvement that is right for you as a beginner. Ideally the professional contacts you will make in the process of engaging in your research and service activities will promote collegiality among librarians locally, nationally, and perhaps even internationally. This can lead to greater professional vision and creativity for you and for your colleagues.

Because it is common for academic librarians to undergo an external review process as part of the reappointment or tenure process, making professional contacts and contributions is important. External reviewers are library or other appropriate professionals from outside your institution who are chosen to evaluate your professional record in an objective manner. They are persons whom you may or may not know. Your institution will have specific guidelines concerning the number of external reviewers needed for a given review, the criteria by which they qualify, and how they are contacted. If you have established a sound record of accomplishments, the external review process will be a favorable experience. One day you may serve as an external reviewer for an academic librarian who is seeking reappointment or tenure.

Another benefit of faculty status is the voice it gives you in faculty governance decisions at your college or university. Working through a primary governing body often called the faculty senate or the faculty assembly, faculty members at colleges and universities work with institutional administrators to formulate scholastic policies as well as standards for faculty appointment, promotion, and tenure. As a faculty member, you will have an opportunity to vote on policy creation or changes. You may also have the opportunity to serve on faculty governance committees or task forces. You may even be eligible to run for an elected faculty office. By participating in faculty governance, you help to influence the intellectual and political direction of your institution.

In addition to obtaining greater job security, if you earn tenure at your institution, you may become eligible for sabbatical leave. If you are granted a sabbatical assignment, you will have paid leave time, usually one semester or one academic year, to pursue your research or professional interests. Once your sabbatical is completed, however, you must demonstrate that you have met the goals as stated in your sabbatical plan.

Drawbacks

Some librarians view the responsibilities associated with academic librarianship as professional drawbacks, particularly those duties linked to tenure track positions including the research and publication requirements of the tenure track system. If for philosophical or other personal reasons you fall into this category, you need to think twice before accepting a faculty librarian position, especially a tenure track position. You must be willing to embrace the responsibilities that come with your faculty appointment, otherwise you are unlikely to succeed in your job. Without a doubt, acquiring tenure is a strenuous process for all faculty members, including faculty librarians.

Under the best of circumstances, there can be pitfalls associated with academic librarianship, particularly where tenure track positions are concerned. Being a tenure track librarian is more than a full-time job. You are sure to experience conflicting demands on your time as you strive to manage your practice of librarianship while at the same time fulfilling your tenure track responsibilities. Some academic libraries provide release time for research and publication, but many do not. There are deadline pressures associated with research and publication. For example, journal and book editors usually impose manuscript submission deadlines. Moreover, you will be working under the pressure of having to produce a sufficient quantity and quality of publications while your tenure clock is ticking.

As a tenure track librarian, you might have difficulties balancing your responsibilities. You may have a tendency to focus on your research and publication requirements at the expense of your traditional librarian responsibilities. However, you cannot neglect your practice of librarianship. It is the performance of those duties such as reference work, technical services work, collection development, and bibliographic instruction that define you as a librarian. The tenure track will demand your engagement in research, publication, service, and creative works, but when you come up for reappointment or tenure review it is likely that your evaluators will weigh your practice of librarianship as heavily, perhaps more heavily, than your other efforts.

If you are a tenure track librarian working in a mixed shop with nontenure track librarians, you might encounter discontent among the nontenure track librarians. They may believe that your tenure track duties place a greater burden upon them to accomplish the service goals of the library. Similarly, you might encounter resentment among support staff if they believe they are doing all the work while you, as a library faculty member, concentrate on research and publication and other professional activities perceived by them as irrelevant to the work of running a library. You could encounter a situation where teaching faculty do not accept you as a true peer. They may resent the fact that you, a librarian with a master's degree, rank among the doctoral degreed professorate as a full-fledged faculty member with all the attenuating rights and privileges. Teaching faculty might also resent the fact that you share the same salary pool with them and thereby compete directly with them for salary and benefit dollars at your institution. More likely, you will experience a higher degree of collegiality with teaching faculty than you would as a librarian without faculty status. Teaching faculty will accept you as a fellow researcher who understands and appreciates their research needs and the research needs of their students.

It is important for you as a faculty librarian to take advantage of opportunities to serve on campus faculty committees or task forces. At many institutions, the teaching faculty will serve on reappointment or tenure review committees for librarian faculty. Working side-by-side with teaching faculty to promote the mission and goals of the institution is a good way to establish rapport with teaching faculty who may make recommendations about your continued employment. Moreover, serving on campus committees is another opportunity for you to fulfill the service expectations of your faculty appointment.

The Future of Faculty Status

There is still heated debate about how well faculty status works for academic librarians. The ACRL is firmly in favor of faculty status for academic librarians, while recognizing that academic status still exists. Ask any academic librarian for an opinion on the topic and you will probably get an earful. In the future, there will still be libraries with all possible permutations of faculty and academic status. At any given institution, it is difficult and takes time to change the system in place. Even if you hear that the status of librarians or the tenure system at a given library is being overhauled, do not start work at an institution expecting the system to change overnight. When librarians have gained faculty status at an institution, staff members may either be "grandfathered" into the system or allowed to keep their jobs without faculty status. Some libraries have both faculty and non-faculty professional librarians. Some universities are creating full-time faculty positions that focus on teaching or "practice" rather than research (Fogg, pp. A12–14). As a librarian, you may have the opportunity to work in this type of position in the future.

The Best Status for You

When you interview for a position, be clear about whether the job carries faculty status or not. Get a copy of the promotion and tenure documentation from the university and the library, review it, and ask questions. You need to know what to do to succeed in that particular system. Ask if you can see samples of actual promotion and tenure dossiers of librarians. Hopefully as part of your interview, you will meet with someone who explains the tenure process to you. If not, ask about it. The process may sound scary but you need to know what you are getting into. Here are other questions to ask: Does a promotion in rank carry a raise in salary with it? How many librarians at the institution are at the various ranks and how many have tenure? How many have lost their jobs in the past because they failed to meet the criteria? How much leave time and financial support are available for research, publication, professional activities, and so on? Do you need a second master's degree or other advanced degrees to earn tenure and/or promotion? Can you stop the tenure clock for personal reasons if necessary?

The key to succeeding in any system is to know the requirements, and faculty status is no different. Before accepting a job, be clear about what you will need to do. For example, one library may base 10 percent of the tenure decision on research and publications while another library bases 40 percent on it. This will make a big difference in your day-to-day work life. Although we can generalize here about some things to look out for, you need to know the requirements at *your* institution. This cannot be stressed too strongly. Know them inside and out. Ask your tenured colleagues for their help and advice, and listen to it. Make a long-range plan of your goals and objectives and stick to it. For example, you might plan to start writing book reviews your first year, then articles for state and regional publications the next year, and a refereed journal article the third year. For more information, Danielle Bodrero Hoggan's 2003 article "Faculty Status for Librarians in Higher Education" offers an extensive overview of issues concerning faculty status.

When considering whether you want a job with faculty status or not, you need to think about what will work best for you. Do you enjoy conducting research, writing articles, and taking part in other scholarly activities? Then you are right for a job with faculty status. If you prefer to put in your eight hours, then go home and never think about work, you may not be cut out for the demands of a tenure track position. However, if you need to find a job in a specific geographic area, you may not have much choice. If your spouse needs to work in Lubbock, Texas, you probably want to find a job in that vicinity. You may care more about living in northern California than about what status you hold at your academic library job. In these cases, be sure you know what you are getting into when you accept a job. Avoid a surprise later, like learning that you are required to have a second master's degree to get tenure and you only have three years left to earn one. Even if you choose a job without faculty status, keep in mind that you may not have the same job for the rest of your life. Most of us change jobs from time to time, and someday you may want or need to take a tenure track job. Remember this as you plan your career and your activities. Keep track of what you have accomplished professionally in case you ever need to create a tenure dossier.

Faculty status may not be the best choice for every academic librarian, but you need to understand what it means. Even if you never have faculty status, some of your colleagues at other schools will. Knowing more about your choices will allow you to make better ones.

Works Cited

"1940 Statement of Principles on Academic Freedom and Tenure with 1970 Interpretive Comments." *American Association of University Professors.* Available: www.aaup.org/statements/Redbook/1940stat.htm

"A report from the Association of College and Research Libraries Task Force on Institutional Priorities and Faculty Rewards, March 1998." *Association of College and Research Libraries. Academic Librarianship and the Redefining of Scholarship Project.* Available: www.ala.org/ACRLPrinter Template.cfm?Section=whitepapers&Template=/ContentManagement/ HTMLDisplay.cfm&ContentID=14974

Association of College and Research Libraries. *1999 Academic Library Trends and Statistics for Carnegie Classification: Doctoral-Granting Institutions, Master's College and Universities, Baccalaureate Colleges.* Chicago: ACRL, 2000.

Boyer, Ernest L. *Scholarship Reconsidered: Priorities of the Professoriate.* Princeton, NJ: The Carnegie Foundation for the Advancement of Teaching, 1990.

Fogg, Piper. "For These Professors, 'Practice' is Perfect." *Chronicle of Higher Education,* 50.32 (2004): A12–14

Hill, Janet Swan. "Wearing Our Own Clothes: Librarians as Faculty." *Journal of Academic Librarianship,* 20 (1994): 71–76

Hoggan, Danielle Bodrero. "Faculty Status for Librarians in Higher Education." *Portal: Libraries and the Academy,* 3 (2003): 431–445.

Massman, Virgil F. *Faculty Status for Librarians.* Metuchen, NJ: Scarecrow Press, 1972.

Vesper, Virginia, and Gloria Kelley. *Criteria for Promotion and Tenure for Academic Librarians.* Chicago: College Libraries Section, ACRL, 1997.

Part 2

**Things to Think About—
Getting and Keeping a Great Job**

CHAPTER 6

"Come on Down! You're the Next Contestant"—One Librarian's View of the Interview Process

Karl Bridges

"You see, I don't believe that libraries should be drab places where people sit in silence, and that's been the main reason for our policy of employing wild animals as librarians."
—Monty Python skit

Everyone wants a good job. The remarkable thing is how badly many people go about it. This chapter will walk the prospective job candidate through the process—from reading the job ad to submitting an application to interviewing to accepting the position. You may have some favorite tricks of your own. By all means, stick with what has worked for you in the past. However, these are some strategies that have worked successfully for me as an applicant, and other librarians I have interviewed as a member of search committees.

First Things First: Finding the Right Opening

First, read the ad carefully. You would be surprised how many applicants miss this basic step. If the position description states that they require five years experience, an advanced degree in science, and fluency in Urdu, do not expect that you, as a new graduate with a BA in Literature, an MLS, no languages, and no experience will be competitive. Do not waste the employer's time or your own. Apply for positions that match your training, talents, and skills. Try to find a job that you will enjoy going to every day. Nothing is worse than having a job you hate, and no amount of salary will make up for that.

69

If you decide to apply, you will need to write a cover letter. Make it a good one. You have, from the time the person opens the envelope, about a minute to interest them in your application. Write a letter that fits the position and shows that you have read the ad and have looked at some background material on the Web site of the school. Try to cover the major requirements in the ad. Keep the letter short, preferably one page. Do not simply rehash the vita; the point of the letter is to get the employer to read your vita.

As a search committee member what I look for is someone who seems to understand the requirements of the position and can articulate to me why they are qualified for the position. I want to know why you, above every other applicant, can do this job better. I am looking for letters that are well written, show good grammar and spelling, and clearly explain to me why I should consider this applicant. I do not want to read a computer generated form letter that has obviously been sent to a hundred other schools. Show me that you care and that you know something about my school and my library. Show sincere interest; demonstrate what you can do for me and my library.

The Vita: Organization, Organization, Organization

The key to a successful professional vita or resume is organization. A resume is a short, usually one page, summary of your job qualifications and experience. A vita (short for curriculum vitae) is a longer document that includes research, presentations, committee work, and other academic activities. As a library professional, you may have a vita of several pages. People on search committees are busy people. They do not have time to hunt through your vita to find information. They want to be able to see the stuff they need to see quickly. This is your first opportunity to present how you do your work. Make it count. What do they want to know? Basically, that you meet the qualifications for the job. This boils down to (a) your experience and (b) your education. In addition, they will be interested in your professional memberships and activities (i.e., ALA, state associations) and your publications. Don't belong to organizations? Join. Don't have any publications? Start writing. If you are a new graduate at least put something on there that indicates that you have an interest in research and publication, such as your thesis or current research interests.

"But the job I want doesn't require publication" mutters the gentle reader. Maybe not, which leads to the next point. Have multiple versions of vitas, and tailor your vita to the job. If the ad stresses teaching, make your vita stress teaching experience. If it stresses publications, emphasize your journal articles. The point of the vita is not just to depict you accurately, but also to serve as an instrument to show the committee that you are, indeed, "their kind of person."

What do search committees not want to know? They have no need to know your age, your marital status, or your sexual orientation. They really do not want to know what fraternity you belonged to or that you were a member of 4-H. Leave off social activities or honors that are questionable in taste or show immaturity. My college used to have an annual festival, now discontinued, that included the crowning of "Miss Watermelon Bust"—a young woman selected for, shall we say, her more obvious physical attributes. Nuf said.

Search committees are not interested in every job that you have had in your life. You are applying for a library job, not filling out an application to work security in a major airport that requires a ten-year history of employment. Show them that you have done library work. The smallest job in a library is better than some nonlibrary job. If you have nonlibrary jobs relevant to the position, by all means include them. Seeing "I was a computer engineer" or "I was a lawyer" is always nice. Include anything that is really interesting and relevant. For example, you may have spent ten years as a Navy SEAL, which shows leadership and organization.

Documenting your education is very important. They want to see your MLS. Tell them what kinds of courses you did in library school. They want to see your graduate degrees and undergraduate majors. If you wrote a thesis for a graduate degree put that in. Grades are an iffy thing. If your grades are good, say in the 3.5 and higher category, you can put them in. On the other hand, if you graduated J.B. (just barely), do not emphasize the fact.

Be prepared to answer questions during the interview about things that are "odd" or "different." I have spent the last fifteen years explaining to search committees why I have two master's degrees in history. (It's nothing bad. Really.) Be prepared to explain gaps in your employment and educational history. Do not give flip answers like "I would have finished my master's thesis, but it was summer and the Sci-Fi Channel was showing a Stargate marathon so …"

Keep your vita focused and on target. Think of it as a marketing tool for an important product—you. Have your finished vita reviewed by someone else—preferably outside your organization. Have them check it for wording, for grammar, for proper punctuation. As the old saw says, you have only one chance to make a first impression.

Proper spelling is only one part of accuracy. The other more important part of accuracy is truthfulness. Resist at all costs the urge to puff up (or outright lie) about your accomplishments. You will be caught eventually, and that is a very bad thing. Do not claim you attended a college or graduated when you did not. The Internet and e-mail makes it too easy to check such things. I could go on about this subject, but the simple fact is that lying is just wrong. It is a bad way to live and a horrible way to start out a relationship with a potential employer, especially if they figure out what you did and wait until the on-campus interview to ask you about it.

Presentation of your vita is important. Take some time and choose an appropriate heavy bond paper. Spend the extra money and have it professionally laser printed. Avoid, at all costs, the urge to be "cute" or "special" or "different." I have seen vitas done in crayon, on pink scented paper, and, I kid you not, as paper cutouts. This just annoys the search committee. Remember that your vita is probably going to be copied and passed around. It needs to project a solid professional image. If you are uneasy about doing it yourself, or you are artistically challenged, have a professional take your information and put it together for you; it is a super investment.

References

References are probably the most important element of getting a new job. After all, these people know you best and can tell the prospective employer about how you are as an employee and a person. Who should be your references? Normally you need three to five references. One of them should be your current supervisor if at all possible; not having your current boss as a reference may raise a red flag. Most bosses are reasonable people who understand that people do move on and will, if not be helpful, at least not be obstructive. Try to talk to your boss as early as possible in the job search process and advise them of what's going on. Let them know when you apply for a job and provide them with a job description so that if someone calls about you, your boss will have a clue about what to tell them.

Your other references are up to you. Try to choose people who know your work and can give good testaments to your ability. Ask people ahead of time to be references—it is the polite thing to do. Try to have more than the minimum number of references so the same person is not called all the time. Fit your references to the position. A music cataloger, for example, would usually be a poor choice for a reference for a science library reference position. In small libraries you cannot always avoid that, but it might help if the reference can really attest to your skills for the position based on their own expertise.

Try to choose as references people who work well with you. If you feel that you have a problem with an individual do not ask them. You want people who can be positive about you. (This does not mean you should choose your best friend, wife, or another person with whom you have a close personal relationship.) What if the person you don't work well with is your boss? In that case, try to have other references that can counterbalance his or her opinion. You might also try to figure out what you are doing that is annoying your boss and fix it, if possible.

When Things Are Bad: If You Were Fired or Turned Down for Tenure

Sometimes you are applying for a job from a position of weakness. You are unemployed or about to be unemployed. Sometimes this is not your fault; your school had a financial crisis and laid off half the library staff. This is an easy one to explain. It happened. It is unfortunate. If, on the other hand, you have been fired for cause, you will need to explain this to your potential employer. You need to be prepared to explain if necessary, (a) what happened, (b) why it happened, and, (c) what you've done to make sure that it will never happen again—ever. My advice: Be honest. Character counts. If you plan to lie, do not bother to apply.

Being turned down for tenure is a particularly difficult situation. Because in most cases tenure is a six or seven year process, it indicates to the prospective employer that you have failed to produce on a fairly long-term basis. Every situation is different. It may be that you did well, but there were only two tenure track slots available in the year you came up for tenure and you didn't make the cut. It may be that you failed to do something that you needed to do, like publish. If you are applying for another tenure track position your failure to make tenure may be an issue. The best policy is honesty. Own both your accomplishments and your lack of accomplishment. If you did not publish, say that was the problem and explain why you did not and what you plan to do differently. In some cases, this can be positive. If you love teaching and didn't publish because you spent all your time in the classroom, a school that emphasizes teaching might see this as a positive, despite your lack of publications. This is a situation where your references will be extremely valuable in explaining the situation.

An alternative situation is that your present job is really a bad situation. You may not get along with your coworkers, your dean may dislike you, you may hate the duties you are assigned, or any combination of these things. The rule in this is simple: No negatives. Period. As a committee and a potential employer, we do not want to hear about it. It's whining and it makes you look bad. Try to stress your positive accomplishments. If the situation is really bad and has negatively impacted your accomplishments at your present job, explain this to the prospective employer: "I am very interested in professional activities, but our dean feels that junior faculty should not be going to conventions and serving on committees and refuses them travel money. I paid to attend the most recent ALA out of my own pocket and took my vacation to do it."

In most cases, however, it is a happier situation. You've done well in your present job and you want to move up in the world, try a different kind of school, try a different region of the country. You may have compelling personal reasons for making a change, like a spouse transferred by their company. Regardless, emphasize that you are *interested in the position*. Do not stress the other nonlibrary elements. For example, I live in Vermont. I do not want to hear in the cover letter or the interview that your primary motivation for wanting a job in my library is that you love snow and want to ski. You are here to be a librarian first and to snowboard second. In the course of the interview it is fine to mention this at an appropriate point, say over dinner (we like people who ski—really), but we do not want it to be the focus of the interview.

Interviewing with Special Circumstances

Other special situations may occur when you are applying for a job. The two most common are probably spousal hires and switching library types/sizes.

You found love. You are blessed. Your love may also share your profession. Double blessing. You both want positions in the same library or at the same institution. Not a blessing. Remember that your loved one, despite how much you care for him or her, is, professionally, a separate person. They need to make their own way. If there are two positions, apply separately. Each of you should expect to be considered on your own merits. If you are offered a position, and your accepting it is contingent on your soul mate's getting a job, bring it up then, but do not make this the first topic of conversation. They are there and you are there to talk about you.

Switching library types is another special situation. People do change, going from public libraries to academic and, less commonly, from academic to public. People also change library size, perhaps going from a small school to a larger university or vice versa. Be prepared to answer questions about why you want to make this change, what skills you have that would be useful in the new environment, and, most importantly, those asked to determine whether you understand the mission and objectives of the role you are being considered for. If you are contemplating a change from Big Research U to Small Church Related College, expect questions about how you will deal with fewer resources. If you are going to a larger school, expect questions about how you plan to deal with increased numbers of students.

Know your audience. Do not, for example, go to a community college interview and stress your research interests and publication record. That's nice, but that's not what they are about. Conversely, do not go to Big Research U and focus on your teaching ability rather than research plans.

The On-Campus Interview

At some point, assuming the stars and planets are aligned correctly, the grand machinery of the library will finish its work and you will be given an on-campus interview. This is good because it means that you are one of the top three or four candidates and have some shot at actually getting the job.

Most people are familiar with the typical one-hour interview for a "regular" job—like being a shop clerk. Academic librarian job interviews are based on a different model: the faculty interview. An interview for a faculty position is different in a variety of ways including length (an academic interview is normally a full day and sometimes two) and comprehensiveness (an academic interview is much more intense than a regular job interview). Colleges and universities are interested in you as a total package, not only how you do the job, but also you as a person and how you will fit into the organization. This can be especially true if you are interviewing at some private colleges with religious ties. In that instance, you can be sure of some probing questions about your faith and your ability/willingness to meet "lifestyle expectations."

The majority of academic librarian interviews require some kind of presentation. In many cases, this is to evaluate your effectiveness as an instructor, say, for a bibliographic instruction position. It is also to give the staff an opportunity to see how you interact with a group under pressure, especially in a larger library where you are not going to have an opportunity to interact with everyone individually. Sad to say, some schools take advantage of the interviewee by requiring some set topic that basically turns your presentation into an in-service training for the staff. I would not take offense at this, but it is something to keep in mind when you are evaluating whether you want the position.

Most people, by the time they have gotten to this stage in life, have some experience with making presentations and doing public speaking. If you don't, get help from friends and colleagues or visit your public library for handbooks. Some advice: (a) have a backup because your computer will fail; (b) try to be interesting and interact with your audience (nothing turns me off more than someone reading from a script); and (c) use PowerPoint judiciously. I realize everyone uses it, but it can be boring. After seeing three or four candidates all having similar looking PowerPoint presentations my eyes (and mind) start to glaze over. If you use it, try to keep your presentation short and the points on each slide to a minimum. Remember, you are there to speak to people—not to mediate between them and some projected slides.

Every interview is different and every school has its own way of doing things. You can generally expect to spend one or two days meeting and talking with lots of people, from campus administrators to library staff to students. There will probably be a formal "interview" where you meet with the search committee and they ask you prepared questions, but there will be other, more informal meetings as well. You may meet dozens of people, but they usually understand that you're seeing many new faces and won't expect you to remember everyone. The following simple do's and don'ts may be useful:

Do's

- Be on time for everything. If you have a cell phone take it with you and if your flight is delayed call the search chair so they know that and someone doesn't have to spend five hours waiting at the airport.

- Do basic maintenance (haircut, shined shoes, dry cleaned suit/professional outfit that fits). Do not let people be distracted by your funky shoes or jewelry. You do not need to look like you stepped out of a fashion magazine, just look your best.

- Take only carry-on luggage. Lost bags are not something you want to deal with.

- Be friendly. Withhold comment on aspects of the library décor, town, restaurant, and so forth, that you do not like. You may think that Hicksville is exactly that, but it is their home.

- If the hotel has a coffeeshop, get up early and have a small breakfast on your own—at your own expense. During the day you will probably be talking during meals and will not be able to finish your food.

- Follow the school's instructions—including about what receipts to keep for reimbursement.

- Make small talk, but avoid controversial subjects like, for instance, the school's ongoing athletic scandal.

- Have some questions for people that show you have a clue. For example, ask how they use online instruction or what changes they have seen at the reference desk due to the use of full-text resources.

Don'ts

- Don't criticize. It is not your library and they may have very good reasons for doing something that you would

not be caught dead doing at your library. Offer
constructive advice when possible.

- You may really disagree with or even take a dislike to
someone, but do not argue with them, especially over
nonlibrary issues (like politics) that may come up.

- Don't ask in large group meetings how the dean is to work
for. It puts people on the spot. Even if the dean is Attila
the Hun reincarnated no one is going to say that openly,
especially to a strange person.

- Watch what you eat and drink. If cabbage or pork or
whatever causes you gas, avoid it. Same for alcohol. You
may normally be fine, but if you are under stress it may
have a different (and stronger) effect on you than usual.

- Avoid fish and stringy pasta (and sauces) if possible. They
are messy.

- If you smoke, quit for the duration of the interview.
Taking smoking breaks is a problem in a tightly
scheduled day.

The most important thing is to be prepared for the unexpected.
Something odd or unexpected will always happen, even if it's nothing
more than a really strange question or an elderly faculty member who
takes the opportunity of your visit to launch into a monologue about
toilets. Seriously. It happened.

Try to be flexible, take the situations and the people you meet with
grace and good humor, and never let them see you sweat. Remember
that you are interviewing the whole time you are with them. I do not
care if it's a walk around campus or you end up drinking beer in the
dean's kitchen. Someone will always be watching and evaluating you.
Don't be paranoid about it, but do try to be on your best behavior.
Even with people you think are tangential to your search process, like
secretaries. In many places, especially small schools, the provost's
secretary can sometimes wield more influence than the library dean.

When Good Interviews Go Bad

The reality is that you cannot usually tell whether a job, the school,
or the people are a good match for you until you get there. You can

think something is really a good situation, arrive and realize that "This is so not going to be happening." There can be many reasons for this on both sides. You may realize early in the interview that the position they are interviewing you for is, in reality, vastly different from what you thought it was when you applied. The school may realize early in the day that you are not a good match for the position. You may simply take an intense dislike to the people, the atmosphere, the building, or something else and realize that you will not take the job. It can be any number of things, most of them not your fault and beyond your control. I have lived close to sea level for my entire life. I went for an interview at a school high in the mountains. I spent three days with altitude sickness. I personally could not have physically taken the job, nice as it was, had they offered it to me. Remember Rule #1: This is business. Don't take it personally.

Your natural impulse when things go bad is to run. Quickly. Away. Don't. The interview is only for one day, sometimes two. The impression you leave with the people lasts much longer. Remember that as a librarian you are seeking a career, not a job. That means that things might change. The director you hate may leave. The ugly building may be renovated. In short, you may meet these people again as a candidate. If not at that school, somewhere else. The library world is small and I can guarantee that you will interact with these people again somewhere: on a committee, at a conference. Why alienate them by being difficult? Be polite, put on your library face, and remember that, even if the situation in that library is horrible, you get to go home. The people interviewing you have to stay there. You can be nice and civil to anyone for one day. Stay focused, stay alert, and try to leave them with the best impression you can. The best thing to do, if people are being jerks, is to be really polite and kind. This reaction confuses them and probably will make them go away in search of other prey.

After the Interview

After you go home, write thank you notes on paper. E-mail is just not the same. Send one to the library director and one to the head of the search committee, thanking him/her and the rest of the committee for the opportunity to meet with them. You do not need to restate your qualifications for the position. This is simply to show that you are a polite caring person.

Send in your reimbursement requests promptly. Use the forms they sent you if they did so. Be neat and accurate. Keep copies for your taxes and in case they lose them. Follow their instructions and figure out exactly what they will reimburse. Asking for money for things that they did not agree to, like your rental car or other extras, will just create bad feelings. Show that you care about their budget.

Now, having done those two things, go do something else. Windsurf, hike, go back to your job and work, or (my personal favorite) to conjugating Attic Greek verbs. Anything, as long as it has nothing to do with the search. Do not worry about when you are going to hear. Do not pester the search committee with e-mail inquiries. Do not call your friend who works at Neighbor U in the same town and ask them to scope out what's going on. Do not moan about your experiences and your chances in the course of your present workday. Nothing is more annoying or more likely to get you rejected, not only from your potential job but also from the one you already have (should you be fortunate enough to have a job already). You did the best you could and the rest is beyond your control. You have bought your lottery ticket and either your number comes up or it doesn't.

Handling Rejection: It's Not You. Really.

If instead of a nice phone call you receive a rejection letter, do not lose heart. The good news is that you probably beat out a big pool of applicants and were their second or third choice. Not bad.

You may not have gotten the job for a whole variety of reasons—many unrelated to your performance. Most schools are extremely fair and try to do the best job they can to be objective. In many cases, it comes down to subjective factors that you have no control over and you may not even be aware of. You are not going to get any responses from the school on why you did not make the cut. Look at it as a learning experience that gave you the opportunity to lift the lid and look inside the library box at another school. Maybe the contents of the box were wonderful and you are disappointed that you did not get in. Maybe you are glad that you were able to shut the lid quickly and nothing escaped.

Don't take it personally. There are always alternatives and choices. What is meant to happen for you will happen in its own time.

"Come on Down," Or, You Got the Job

If you got the job offer, congratulations! From here on in you should have smooth sailing. In some cases there is very little to negotiate. The issues of salary, moving expenses, professional expenses may have been dealt with in the interview, or it may be that you have to deal with these issues now. Just remember to be realistic; if the job was advertised at $30,000 you are not going to get $50,000 out of them. Be reasonable and remember that you will have to work with these people for, hopefully, many years.

During the interview, assuming that everything went well, it is perfectly reasonable (and expected) that the issue of salary is discussed, especially if it was not mentioned in the ad. Usually this happens at the end of the interview when you are meeting with the director or dean. Once you have an offer, use what you learned in these general discussions to negotiate a salary that works for you. I have seen a range of behavior from directors on the issue of salary from being very honest about what they can afford to those who were obvious skinflints primarily interested in getting someone for the cheapest possible price. The thing to keep in mind is this: If you feel your potential employer is not treating you fairly in terms of salary, can you expect them to be fair in other areas of your work life? If you go into a job feeling you have been robbed financially, it will have an impact on your attitude toward the work. Then again, money is not everything, so you will have to figure out what is most important to you.

You can and should take a reasonable amount of time, several days, to decide what you want to do about a job offer. At this point, I can't give you any more advice. You have seen the situation, you know the facts. Follow your heart.

CHAPTER 7

Mentors—How To Find Them, How To Use Them

Verla J. Peterson

"Keep away from people who try to belittle your emotions. Small people always do that, but the really great make you feel that you, too, can become great."
—Mark Twain

I remember the doubt and fear that I experienced as the end of library school drew near and I contemplated what it would be like to actually be out of school and be *a librarian at last!* I think back to a conversation I had during that time with my graduate school advisor at the University of Wisconsin, Dr. Wayne Wiegand. I had done fine in my classes and had enjoyed several brief stints at student and para-professional positions in different libraries. I was concerned never-theless that I would not know what to do once I got into that first job. Uncle Wayne, as we affectionately called him, put me at ease.

"Peterson, believe me, you've got everything it takes," he said. "You'll be fine." Today, with fifteen years of hindsight, I can see that he was right. Moreover, all these years later, I think that simple exchange exemplifies one of the most important roles that a mentor can take: to believe in the mentee, and to express that confidence to them.

Why Have a Mentor?

Like most professions, ours is one where we largely learn by doing. Our education provides a theoretical and philosophical grounding for accessing and organizing information, for the importance of intellectual freedom and equality of access to our profession, for managing a library, and for some of the basic skills of public and technical services work. Nonetheless, the master's degree barely scratches the surface of what a seasoned librarian needs to know to do high-quality work. Every new librarian faces a steep learning curve. Experienced librarians face times in their careers when they need to learn the culture of a new organization or develop a new skill set. In these situations, a mentor can help you shorten the learning curve.

Although they may be especially important at the beginning, mentors meet a variety of needs as your career progresses. Studies have shown a host of benefits to those who have the guidance of a mentor. The advantages include higher salaries, career satisfaction, and satisfaction with the organization (Munde, p. 172), as well as the opportunity to take concerns to someone for comments without exposing those concerns to a larger part of the organization (Roberts, p. 118). As you move through your career, mentors can help you adjust more quickly to a new environment, enhance your career development, learn or improve a specific skill, or gain understanding about what is considered important at your library (Kahn). They can also help you to identify opportunities for expanding your professional network, developing your career in a way that may help you move on to a position that offers new challenges, or gain a promotion where you are (Nankivell).

This last role will certainly be important to librarians who are in tenure track positions. Many new faculty members report that they receive little formal information regarding the tenure process, and describe it as "ambiguous, uncertain, and stressful" (Mullen and Forbes, p. 34). A mentor can help you understand not only the mechanics of what is required for obtaining tenure in your institution, but also the less tangible political milieu that surrounds the process in your particular environment.

The fact that mentors can serve different purposes means that there may not be just one person in your life or your career who becomes The Mentor. One definition of mentoring is "learning by association with a relevant role model" (Fisher). As an academic librarian, you may want to pursue a mentoring relationship with more than one person to aid you in developing different skills. For example, you could work with one colleague whose instructional skills are excellent in order to improve your teaching, and another who is adept at management to develop your supervisory skills. You may also form a series of bonds over the years, learning from different people as their expertise and support become relevant to you at different times.

I can identify at least half a dozen people who have served as mentor figures to me over the course of my career; I expect there will be more. In my first professional position, I found myself in a one-person library with lots of questions and no one at hand to answer them. The supervisors from the student position I had in library school graciously got me through the first weeks of that job, fielding phone calls from me almost every day. A few years later, after working in reference and interlibrary loan, I realized I had an interest in library administration. I moved to a new state and a new job, where I believed the director would serve as a mentor for me in learning to be a strong and compassionate leader and manager. (She did—thanks, Carol!) Soon after I started in my current position, we began planning to move our library to a new space to be renovated to our specifications. I worked with a retired library director with a Ph.D. in library architecture. He helped me make my way through piles of floor plans and the labyrinth of decisions to be made about HVAC, wiring, lighting, and furnishings. In each case, I moved further and faster than I ever could have without the support and guidance these mentors gave me.

Getting Your Mentor

So where can you find a mentor, the person who can help you to grow personally and professionally and advance in your career? There are many possibilities, ranging from formal programs sponsored by organizations to informal matching where the mentor and mentee are self-selected. Your library may have a program whereby all new librarians are matched with a more experienced colleague to help them learn about the institution and, if applicable, to help them make their way successfully through the tenure process.[1] You may even be fortunate enough to land a residency that includes mentoring as an aspect of the experience.

If you do not find yourself in one of these situations, many other programs match mentees with possible mentors. Here are some possibilities to explore:

- National association sponsored programs, such as ALA
  New Members Round Table, ACRL's E. J. Josey Spectrum

Scholar Mentoring Program, the American Association of Law Libraries mentoring program, or programs offered by the ALA ethnic caucuses

- Your state library association
- Your university alumni association
- Your library school alumni association
- Diversity Librarians Network, coordinated by staff at the University of Tennessee-Knoxville (www.lib.utk.edu/residents/dln)

However, there are some people (and I am among them) who believe that you are most likely to find a successful match with a mentor through informal channels. The mentor–mentee relationship is very personal and can deal with some intimate and intense issues. It is essential that you trust and admire your mentor and that you feel comfortable sharing your doubts and foibles. You will want to look for someone who has a level of self-awareness and who will encourage self-reflection on your part. The potential mentor should be a good listener and adept at giving honest, challenging feedback in a constructive way. The person should be confident but not egotistical, or they, rather than your growth, will be the focus of your conversations. They should be nonjudgmental and respectful. A sense of humor is definitely a plus!

The logical place to start in searching for possible mentors is to look around at your colleagues. Is there someone in your library who does things in a way you find admirable? Someone who exhibits skills (professional, political, or interpersonal) that you would like to master? Someone you perceive as adept at coaching and teaching others? Consider approaching that person once or twice for some advice to see whether you think the pairing might work for a more extensive mentoring relationship.

Remember that, although a librarian at a peer or higher level is most likely to know about areas you want to pursue, many people have valuable life experience to share. In my first administrative position, there was a library technician in our cataloging department who was a retired navy ship captain. He had run a small floating city and commanded 400 sailors; he knew something about management! I had more than one conversation with him where he advised and encouraged me as I got my "sea legs" as a director.

Other possibilities in surveying the landscape for an informal mentor figure include continuing a relationship with one of your graduate school professors, maintaining contact with someone you met in a practicum or pre-MLS position, approaching someone in your community or social circle who has characteristics you want to emulate, or pursuing further contact with someone you meet online (for example, through a professional discussion list). I find this last possibility extremely interesting. Although I don't believe it would work very well for me personally as a high-touch, face-to-face type, some people might find the distance involved in "e-mentoring" actually helps them to open up and share in a way that would be intimidating in person. One experiment that matched library school students with experienced librarians for a semester reported that the "facelessness" of online mentoring wasn't a problem; in some cases, it helped students who were reluctant to ask for advice to approach their mentors more easily (Henderson, p. 161). You may find yourself clicking with someone you encounter online in a way that has not happened with any of your on-site colleagues. If you notice someone on a discussion list who consistently posts things that resonate with you, contact them off-list and strike up a conversation (Brookover).

Mentors are especially important for the success and upward career mobility of women and minorities.[2] In recent years women have begun to be much better represented in the upper levels of library organizations, but the profession is still struggling to recruit and support the development of enough librarians of color to serve adequately the diverse populations that surround us. Tracie Hall, Director of the ALA Office for Diversity, believes that one of the most empowering activities you can undertake is to choose a mentor for yourself. She recommends, however, that you consider selecting a mentor "who might not look just like you." Hall, an African American woman, identifies a white male as the primary mentor figure in her professional life thus far. Her advice is to select a mentor who is doing what you might like to be doing about ten years down the road. "A mentor who is different from you can enlarge your view of the profession and bring you into their larger circle," resulting in a richer experience, Hall says.

One caveat is necessary here as I discuss ways of finding a potential mentor. Although it may seem that your supervisor is well situated to observe your work and give you feedback, thus putting him or her at the perfect vantage point for mentoring you, the purposes of the supervisory and mentoring roles can sometimes conflict, putting you both in an awkward situation. In fact, in some organizations that have formal mentoring programs, the mentor and mentee are required to be outside the direct reporting line from each other. If you develop a strong mentoring relationship with your boss, others can perceive it as favoritism (Harris, p. 38; Brookover). Negotiating a disagreement can also be tricky if you have both a reporting and a mentee relationship with someone (Shontz, p. 124). Sometimes the issue you need mentoring on is how to deal with that very same boss; you can see the inherent conflict here. There may also be things about yourself you are uncomfortable sharing with your supervisor, and this can impede the development of the openness and trust that is so vital to a successful mentoring relationship. For all these reasons—confidentiality, openness, and safety—you may want to look outside your department, or even outside your organization, for an appropriate mentor figure. This does not mean a supervisor should never take on a mentor role for you. However, if this happens, proceed with caution.

Developing a Relationship with Your Mentor

Once you find that person whom you believe will serve as a good mentor figure for you, it is helpful to know some of the elements necessary in successful mentoring relationships. The bottom lines are mutual respect, commitment to the process, and interest in the relationship being a two-way learning process (Kahn). These elements are largely assured by selecting someone whose personal qualities lend themselves well to the mentoring relationship. It is also important to agree on a structure for your interactions (Nankivell). Discuss early on how frequently you will meet and how long the meetings will be. Will they be set up in advance on a regular schedule, or will you schedule meetings more spontaneously? Be flexible and respectful of your mentor's time.

Both the mentor and the mentee should be clear about the objectives of the relationship. Before you approach someone as a potential mentor, you should put considerable thought into what you would like to learn and what skills you are currently trying to improve in your professional life. Discuss these things with your prospective mentor. This will set the tone for later conversations, and will keep you both focused on goals for your periodic meetings. It is also help-ful to keep notes or a journal about your conversations with your mentor, and to have a check-in conversation occasionally where you revisit and update the objectives that you set out in the beginning.[3]

In addition to meeting and talking, there are many things that you and your mentor can do together to promote your learning. Kahn offers a nice list, including seeing a speaker together, engaging in job shadowing, serving on a task force or committee together, and hold-ing a mock job interview. In the academic environment, a mentor might observe your teaching and give you responses, give input on research you are conducting, or help refine an article before you sub-mit it for peer review.

A mentor can help you to build a professional network by intro-ducing you to others or by having you come along to functions where you make contacts. I recently served as a mentor for a student at the Information School of the University of Washington. She currently works at Amazon.com and wanted to explore career options, espe-cially with technology vendors who serve libraries. It took just a cou-ple of telephone calls to set up meetings for her with representatives from a major database vendor and a Seattle-based library-oriented software company. She described these visits as valuable in helping her shape her career path. Afterwards, we met and discussed what she had observed and learned.

Up to this point, I have talked about the mentoring process almost entirely from the mentee's perspective. However, serving as a mentor also brings a host of benefits to those who are willing and able to ded-icate the time and energy to the process. As a mentor, you are likely to see your work with a fresh eye and to benefit from the energy the mentee brings to his or her relatively new position. You may feel a renewal of professional purpose, or gain information about emerging aspects of the profession that a new librarian studied in his or her graduate work (Munde, p. 172). Many individuals move into formal or informal mentoring roles because they have the experience and per-sonal qualities that encourage others to seek them out, or because they want the satisfaction of influencing future professionals. It is as important for the mentor to dedicate time and thought to the process as it is for the mentee.[4]

I have moved into the stage of my career where I am a mentor more often than a mentee. I find it very important to view myself as a co-explorer and a facilitator for learning, rather than someone who is there primarily to dispense wisdom. The relationships I have with various librarians—some brand new to the profession, some mid-career, and some veterans—all teach me different things. The biggest benefit is maintaining a flexible, learning-focused mindset even well into my career. As I explore possibilities with mentees, I remember that I am involved in an adventure. Life is a long learning process where we never arrive at perfection, but are always moving forward. Although it may sound clichéd, in my experience it really *is* about the journey and not the destination.

Over and above the advantages to individuals, there are definite benefits to both the organization and the profession in fostering mentoring relationships. Institutions with successful mentoring programs typically experience increased retention and reduced turnover, as well as gaining from the increased efficiency of employees who are inducted more quickly into the norms and performance expectations of the organization (Munde, p. 172). Being mentored may also reduce burnout by giving librarians support, cross training, and variety in their work (Golian and Galbraith, p. 115). Most important to me, however, is the long-term benefit that mentoring can provide to the profession of librarianship. For some years, we have realized that the next decades will bring a shortage of librarians as those who entered the profession in the 1960s and 1970s retire. The situation is worsened by the smaller number of graduates entering the field, and by the number of people who decide to leave librarianship for other careers. The forthcoming deficit will be felt especially strongly in leadership positions. Library director positions are becoming increasingly difficult to fill.

Developing a culture of mentorship and learning throughout our library culture will go a long way toward retaining the talented Nexgen professionals who are now entering the field and fostering the leaders of tomorrow. Such leaders will be needed to take us forward in a challenging climate of constant change. If you are interested in working in a vital and growing profession, I have one last piece of advice: Seek out a mentor today, but become one tomorrow.

Endnotes

1. For a description of one such program at Indiana University, see www. indiana.edu/~libpers/mentor.html.

2. For discussion of this assertion, see Munde, p. 172; Jones-Quartey, p. 27; Turock, p. 120; Harris, pp. 37–38; Kirkland, p. 376; and Hardy, p. 11.
3. For additional exercises for maximizing the mentee experience, see Cohen's *Mentee's Guide* and Shea.
4. For a useful overview of mentoring behaviors and discussion approaches, see Cohen's *Manager's Pocket Guide.*

Works Cited

Brookover, Sophie. "Mentors: What Are They Good For?" *The Library & Information Science Professional's Career Development Center.* December 2003. n. pag. Online. Available 13 July 2004: www.liscareer.com/brookover _mentoring.htm

Cohen, Norman H. *The Manager's Pocket Guide to Effective Mentoring.* Amherst, MA: HRD Press, 1999.

Cohen, Norman H. *The Mentee's Guide to Mentoring.* Amherst, MA: HRD Press, 1999.

Fisher, Biddy. "Do As I Do." *Library Association Record*, October 1997. n. pag. Online. Available 11 July 2004: www.la-hq.org.uk/directory/record/r19

Golian, Linda Marie, and Michael W. Galbraith. "Effective Mentoring Programs for Professional Library Development." *Advances in Library Administration and Organization*, 14 (1996): 95–124.

Hall, Tracie. Telephone interview. 13 July 2004.

Hardy, Letty C. "Mentoring: A Long-Term Approach to Diversity." *HR Focus*, 75 (1998): 11.

Harris, Roma M. "The Mentoring Trap." *Library Journal*, 118 (October 15, 1993): 37–39.

Henderson, Kathryn Luther. "Electronic 'Keyboard Pals': Mentoring the Electronic Way." *Serials Librarian*, 29 (1996): 141–164.

Jones-Quartey, Theo. "Mentoring—Personal Reflections of a Special Librarian." *Information Outlook*, 4 (July 2000): 26–30.

Kahn, Linda. *Is It Mentoring or Is It Magic?* 1998. Online. Available 11 July 2004: www.sla.org/chapter/ctor/events/mentoring

Kirkland, Janice. "The Missing Women Library Directors: Deprivation Versus Mentoring." *College & Research Libraries*, 58 (July 1997): 376–384.

Mullen, Carol A., and Sean A. Forbes. "Untenured Faculty: Issues of Transition, Adjustment and Mentorship." *Mentoring & Tutoring*, 8 (2000): 31–46.

Munde, Gail. "Beyond Mentoring: Toward the Rejuvenation of Academic Libraries." *Journal of Academic Librarianship*, 26 (2000): 171–175.

Nankivell, Clare. "Essentials of a Good Relationship." *Library Association Record*, October 1997. n. pag. Online. Available 11 July 2004: www.la-hq. org.uk/directory/record/r199710/nanki.html

Roberts, Deanna L. "Mentoring in the Academic Library." *College & Research Libraries News*, 47 (February 1986): 117–119.

Shea, Gordon F. *Making the Most of Being Mentored: How to Grow from a Mentoring Partnership*. Menlo Park, CA: Crisp Learning, 1999.

Shontz, Priscilla K. *Jump Start Your Career in Library and Information Science*. Lanham, MD: Scarecrow Press, 2002.

Turock, Betty J. "Women and Leadership." *Journal of Library Administration*, 32 (2001): 111–132.

CHAPTER 8

Continuing Education— Planning Your Future

Kris Swank

"Who dares to teach must never cease to learn."
—John Cotton Dana (1856–1929)

"Our library degree gets us in the door. But that is really just the beginning," says Susanne Markgren, a librarian at Mount Sinai School of Medicine in New York City. "Librarianship itself is one long learning process—with no end in sight. ... Our profession is in a constant state of flux, and, therefore, so are the roles that librarians play (par. 1)." A rapidly changing environment is just one reason to consider continuing education at any stage of your career. Other reasons vary from accomplishing personal goals to advancing in the organization and changing jobs.

Definitions of continuing education vary by institution and state, but the Oklahoma Department of Libraries gives a good basic one: continuing education is "a lifelong learning process which builds on and modifies previously acquired knowledge, skills and attitudes of the individual (par. 6)." Continuing education includes a wide variety of learning activities, including in-service education, credit and non-credit courses, seminars, workshops, training programs, and attendance at professional conferences. A related term is "professional development," which also includes activities where the librarian is the disseminator of knowledge, such as research, publishing papers, presenting at conferences, sabbatical projects, fellowships, and teaching. (For more on these activities see the chapters on research and service.)

Throughout this chapter, you will learn tips and tricks for finding the right continuing education opportunities and for making them enjoyable as well as educational.

You Will Need Continuing Education

There are many reasons that continuing education is important to academic librarians and should form a continuous part of your professional life. In library literature, the most frequently mentioned reasons include updating skills, accomplishing personal goals, advancing in the organization, and changing careers.

"When I started as a librarian, they hadn't even invented that yet."

"Change has become the norm rather than the exception," explains Deborah S. Grealy, Director of the Library and Information Science Program at the University of Denver (p. 6). She cites a theory, developed by Peter Vaill, that rapidly changing technology in libraries has created a "permanent whitewater" situation. This condition, Grealy says, where a work environment is constantly in motion, "forces the members of organizations to continually do things they have little or no experience doing. This means that, in addition to acquiring new skills and attitudes, library employees have to learn to be more effective learners" (p. 6).

"When I became a library director in 1989, we had one computer," says Susan Bledsoe, about Thunderbird—The American Graduate School of International Management in Glendale, Arizona. "It was locked away in a small office because it cost hundreds of dollars per hour to access the databases. Over the next five years, our library underwent an information technology revolution. Every staff member got a PC on her desk, and our patrons were provided with rows of computers connected to e-mail, the World Wide Web, and dozens of databases free for them to use." Of course, library school had not trained her to use all this technology; it had not existed then. Therefore, Bledsoe and her staff incorporated continuing education into their annual routine. "We attended a steady stream of workshops and seminars. We had to, in order to stay up-to-date."

In the 1990s, libraries began offering remote access to databases. By 2004, many were going wireless. Each technological advance has brought a whole new set of questions from users, and librarians have been expected not only to find information but to know how to operate the technology as well. Continuing education is critical for librarians to keep pace with changing technologies, resources, and even clientele.

"When I got hired, they didn't tell me I'd be doing this."

Library school may not have prepared you for all your job duties. Many library schools do not offer training in specific job functions like repairing books, claiming missing issues of serials, managing student aides, or complying with government regulations. Continuing education can help you fill those skill gaps. Local and regional organizations, like Amigos Library Services (www.amigos.org) or your regional OCLC service provider, furnish a wide range of seminars and training workshops designed to teach these important daily tasks.

"I've always wanted to learn Spanish!"

Most librarians are naturally life-long learners. Our innate curiosity and passion for knowledge got us into the profession in the first place. Many librarians use continuing education to keep their brains well oiled and their careers interesting. As a plus, whatever we learn usually comes in handy on the job. Whether you are interested in accounting, learning another language, or rock climbing, continuing education can help you contribute to your organization while meeting your own personal goals. Taking an accounting class can help you develop the budget of the library. Learning a new language will make you more valuable at the reference desk or in cataloging non-English materials. Learning to rock climb as a group can help your library staff develop problem-solving skills and build a tightly knit team. You and your organization always get something back from continuing education.

In my own job as a librarian at a business school, the administration offered to pay my tuition for one management class each semester. Although I had never considered getting a business degree before, it turned out to be a win–win situation: I earned a second Master's degree, and the school got a long-term, highly specialized employee. They knew I would not leave my job during the six years it took me to earn the degree, and I was better able to help the students because I had taken the same classes and completed the same assignments.

"I've already been hired. Now I have to prove myself all over again?"

Teachers, doctors, and many other professionals have specific continuing education requirements for recertification in their profession. Although there are no national standards for academic librarians, completing a certain amount of continuing education or professional development may be required for you to get a raise, move up the organizational ladder, or earn tenure. Requirements vary among libraries. "You can move up the salary schedule by earning additional graduate-level credits," says Nancy Buchanan, a librarian at Pima Community College in Tucson, Arizona, "but we aren't required to have tenure." Across town, at the University of Arizona's Health Sciences Center, librarians do earn tenure, which they call "continuing status." According to Patricia A. Auflick, Outreach Services Librarian there, "We have a general guideline of 80 percent job performance, 10 percent scholarship, and 10 percent professional services."

If continuing education or professional development is required at your institution, find out which activities will fulfill the requirements. At some schools, attending a professional conference is sufficient. Other institutions require that you actually present a paper or poster session at the conference in order to receive professional development credit. Ask for specific requirements at an institution before you accept a job offer or sign a contract. Once you start working, even if tenure is years away, do not wait. "You may as well start to focus your continuing education activities right away," advises Brooke Sheldon, recently retired Director of the University of Arizona's School of Information Resources and Library Science. "Remember the old saying, 'the journey of 1,000 miles begins with a single step.'"

"It's time to move on."

It may not be required in your current job, but a solid record of continuing education can help you get your next one. Hiring committees want to see librarians who have regularly updated their skills. Also, if you move to a tenure track position from a nontenure track one, having some continuing education in the bank, so to speak, may help you earn tenure more quickly or easily.

If you decide to leave the field of librarianship, continuing education may prepare you for your next career move. When Nicole Tassinari wanted to change careers, she used the extensive continuing education she had received as a librarian as a selling point. "During my interview for a job as staff consultant with one of the Big Six consulting firms in Washington D.C., a senior partner kept using finance terms I didn't understand. When I had to admit my ignorance, he said that was fine. He could teach me about revenues, expenses, and formulas. What he couldn't teach were the analytical and research skills I'd developed from years of training on databases like LexisNexis and Dialog. Those were the skills he really wanted, and I got the job."

Make a Plan

Now you are convinced you need to include some continuing education in your professional life. The next step is to make a plan. Some organizations require you to establish professional goals for your probationary review or annual evaluation. Even if your institution does not require one, a continuing education plan will serve as a roadmap, guiding you to a specific destination. Write your plan down and keep it in a folder along with your current job description and updated resume. Refer to it at least once a year, and revise it as your needs and desires change.

Through the remainder of this chapter, you will move through the steps of developing your own continuing education plan. Start by setting your goals for continuing education, and identifying the skills you still need to acquire to achieve those goals.

Continuing Education Plan: Your Skills Gaps

1. What goals do you have for your current position?

2. Do you lack, or need to update, any skills to accomplish those goals?

3. What would you like your next career move to be?

4. What skills do you need to move into that position?

5. Which of those skills do you lack (or need to update)?

6. What skills, not specifically related to your job, do you want to learn?

7. Rank, in order of priority, the skills you need/want to acquire.

Next, decide how much time and effort you are willing or able to commit to continuing education and what modes of instruction might be right for you. Continuing education can include anything from a one-hour seminar on book repair to a five-year doctoral degree program. Additionally, new technologies now allow you to choose from myriad instructional modes, from traditional classroom lectures to Web-based courses.

If you're interested in taking a Web-based class, Christine Hamilton-Pennell, owner of Mosaic Knowledge information consultancy, has the following suggestions (p. 35):

- Find out how much time the course is expected to take.

- Determine what kind of classroom interaction is comfortable for you: Do you need a more structured environment? Are you an independent learner?

- Preview the course syllabus and required readings to make sure they will meet your learning needs.

- Find out how much technical support is available for the course.

Many online courses will use a commercial classroom software package, such as WebCT or Blackboard. Contact the instructor or administrator a few weeks before the course begins and ask if you will need any prior training to use the software, or if you will need any equipment in addition to a personal computer and an Internet connection. Determining your personal preferences is an important step in finding the right continuing education program for you.

Find Opportunities

Locating continuing education opportunities is easy. You need look no further than your local library school or professional organization. However, you can also look as far afield as the whole wide world. Following are some organizations and Web sites for you to investigate. When you find a continuing education site that you want to revisit, save it under "Bookmarks" or "Favorites" on your Web browser. You may want to create a subfolder for your personal list of continuing education sites.

National and international library associations usually have continuing education programs, but don't forget to check with your local, state, or regional library organization for any workshops, seminars, or programs that they sponsor. A good example is the Arizona Library Association's Web site (http://www.azla.org), which maintains a calendar of continuing education opportunities in Arizona and beyond. Find your library association's Web site on these useful lists:

- The American Library Association's list of American state and regional library associations (www.ala.org/ala/ ourassociation/ chapters/stateandregional/ stateregional.htm)

- The School of Library and Information Science at San Jose State University's international list of Professional Associations in the Information Sciences (slisweb.sjsu.edu/resources/orgs.htm)

Most library conferences offer continuing education courses, seminars, or workshops in conjunction with their annual meetings. Check the conference's Web site for a list of continuing education opportunities, or call, write, or e-mail the conference registrar to ask for a copy of the program. At many conferences, you must register for continuing education sessions well in advance of the conference. For listings of upcoming library conferences, visit these pages:

- The American Library Association's Events & Conferences Web page (www.ala.org/ala/events/eventsconferences.htm)

- Douglas Hasty's Library Conference Planner (www.fiu. edu/~hastyd/lcp.html)

Many library schools offer mid-career education for their alumni and other professionals, or you can just take a regular library school class. Many courses are now online, so you can participate in a class without leaving your office. For instance, the School of Library and Information Studies at the University of Wisconsin-Madison offers a number of virtual and distance courses, study tours, and summer camps for practicing professionals (www.slis.wisc.edu/academic/ ces/index.html). If your library school does not offer any mid-career education, ask them to add it. They may consider offering a workshop or two at homecoming, over the summer, or online. Find links to library school Web sites on these pages:

- The American Library Association's list of Accredited Programs (www.ala.org/ala/education/accredprograms/ accreditedprograms.htm)

- The School of Library and Information Science at San Jose State University's list of Library Schools in the United

States and Canada (slisweb.sjsu.edu/resources/
libraryschools.htm)

- InformationR.net's World List of Departments and
  Schools of Information Studies (informationr.net/wl)

Many state libraries sponsor continuing education opportunities.
For example, the State of Michigan's Department of History, Arts and
Libraries (http://www.michigan.gov/hal) lists dozens of opportunities under "For the Professional." Find your state library Web site
here:

- The Library of Congress's list of State Libraries
  (lcweb.loc.gov/global/library/statelib.html)

If your library is a member of a consortium, it may sponsor continuing education opportunities, like the Utah Academic Library
Consortium (www.ualc.net). Regional library services providers, such
as Amigos Library Services (www.amigos.org) in the southwestern
U.S., typically offer dozens of useful workshops. OCLC, the world-
wide library cooperative, lists training seminars and other events by
topics or region (www.oclc.org/education). The OCLC site also provides a map and links to all the U.S. regional service providers.

Dialog (www.dialog.com) and LexisNexis (lexisnexis.com/custserv/
training) are just two of the many database providers that offer additional training on their products. Check the Web sites or monthly
newsletters for the training schedules of any vendors with which your
library has an account. There are also meta-lists of training and educational opportunities that you can bookmark on your computer.
One of the best is the Central Colorado Library System's "Directory of
Online Library-Related Courses" (www.cclsweb.org). It lists training
and events nationwide. The World Wide Web is a great place to find
tutorials on any number of subjects. TILT—the Texas Information
Literacy Tutorial (tilt.lib.utsystem.edu)—is a self-paced instructional
module that may be helpful to students as well as new library hires.
Use a search engine like Google (www.google.com) or Yahoo! (www.
yahoo.com) to find other tutorials on specific topics.

Brooke Sheldon smiles and says, "You can learn just as well in
Santa Barbara as in Deadwood." Many academic institutions offer
their librarians professional development funds for approved travel

Continuing Education Plan: Your Program Preferences

1. Will you need to complete a certificate or degree to earn these skills?

2. How many hours/days/years can you devote to acquiring these skills?

3. How many hours per week can you spend on continuing education (and homework, if applicable)?

4. Do you have any special blocks of time you can devote to continuing education (i.e., lunch hours, evenings, weekends, summers, sabbaticals, etc.)?

5. Are you an independent learner, or do you prefer more structured learning environments?

6. What technology do you have available?

   - computer connected to the Internet at work and /or at home

   - fax machine

   - teleconferencing

   - video conferencing

7. Rank the modes of instructional delivery you prefer:

   - traditional classroom lecture

   - evening or weekend classes

   - self-paced independent classes

   - workshops of two days or less

   - telecourses/video courses

   - online instruction

and education. Moreover, because not every subject you want to study will be offered in your neighborhood, you may be able to travel to a national or international site. This can turn out to be quite a nice benefit. If your seminar is in Paradise on a Friday, you might be able to combine business with pleasure. As long as you pay for any unofficial expenses yourself (such as extra hotel nights and food) and take the appropriate vacation days, some institutions will allow you to stay longer and enjoy a mini-break. Check with your institution for their specific rules.

Continuing Education Plan: Your Information Resources

List specific Web sites or links to continuing education listings that you find useful or interesting.

- National and international library associations

- Local, state, and regional library associations

- Favorite library conferences

- Library schools—your alma mater and others

- Your state library

- Consortia to which your library belongs

- Commercial vendors to which your library subscribes

- States and countries you want to visit

- Library associations and conferences in those locales

- Other interesting Web sites

If you still can't find the type of continuing educational opportunity you are seeking, why not create your own? You have already determined your "skills gaps," now examine your "skills sets." Even if you are new to the field, you may have something to teach your peers. Perhaps you just graduated from library school and know more about a hot new technology than more seasoned professionals who have not seen the inside of a classroom for years. What do you know that others might like to learn? Offer to teach a class, present a paper, or conduct a poster session.

If you don't want to teach a subject yourself, but you wish it were being taught in your area, invite an expert to deliver a presentation at your institution or local professional conference. Contact authors of books and articles you find intriguing. Review other conference proceedings and find experts who have already delivered presentations on topics of interest. They may be ready to come and deliver presentations in your area on short notice. Contact your local library association to learn about their procedures for inviting guest speakers to conferences.

Continuing Education Plan: Your Skill Sets

Organize this information about yourself:

- Your areas of expertise

- Your personal interests

- Classes you took at library school that practicing professionals may have missed (such as new technologies)

- Names of experts or authors you know or would like to contact

- Organizations that may sponsor a continuing education opportunity you want to deliver or arrange

---

Make It Happen

The next step is to investigate your institution's policies regarding professional development and continuing education funds for librarians. Do all librarians share a common pool of money, or does each librarian receive a certain amount each year? Can you roll the funds over from year to year, or do unused funds revert to the general college fund at the end of each fiscal year? Get the policies in writing before you embark on a time-consuming and costly program.

Which activities will qualify for professional development and continuing education funds? Some institutions allow you to spend funds for virtually any learning activity. Others will only pay for a conference if you are contributing a paper or poster session, not just attending. Some institutions will help you pay for continuing education that leads to a higher degree. Others will not pay for continuing education that you want to apply toward raises and promotions. Next, find out if your organization has any rules concerning travel, especially international travel, on school business. Can you use professional development and continuing education funds for overseas travel? Do you have to get it approved in advance? How far in advance? And what paperwork needs to be completed and signed?

If you are seeking a new job, an appropriate time to inquire about continuing education and professional development funds, according to Brooke Sheldon, is about three-quarters of the way through the interview process: after your initial round or two of interviews, but before you accept the job or sign a contract. If you are uncomfortable discussing financial topics with your potential new boss, discuss them with a Human Resources or Benefits officer. It is their job to understand and explain these policies to new hires, and they will not think it's peculiar if you ask detailed, pointed questions.

In most academic institutions, continuing education and professional development funds are governed by set policies, with no room for negotiation. In tight budget years, they tend to be among the first items cut. So even if the continuing education/professional development package looks fabulous when you are hired, there is no guarantee it will still be there after the next budget crunch. Always be prepared to throw in some of your own money. You may have to cover part of the travel, food, or lodging expenses. You may have to let your school's designated travel agent book tickets for you. Their job is to get the school the cheapest airline tickets, which usually means red eye flights and multiple stopovers. Some institutions will let you keep any frequent flier miles you accrue on school business, whereas others will keep the miles in the school's account. If your institution has a travel office or designated travel agent, ask them about specific travel policies.

If you are already working at a library, talk with a colleague who has been through the process before, and make a friend in the Business Office of your school. These two valuable people can give you advice and walk you through the necessary steps and paperwork for getting your continuing education approved and paid for.

Once you have found the right program to match your personal and professional goals, and it meets your institution's basic criteria, you still might have to sell it to your supervisor (or someone even higher up). In order for that to happen, you will need to mesh your goals with those of your library or organization. Maybe you have decided that next November it is vital you attend a workshop on "Improving the Reference Interview" in the Bahamas. (It could happen.) Here's your best shot at making it work: Find the intersection between your desires and your organization's goals. Has your supervisor been encouraging staff to improve performance at the reference desk? Does your college or university have any exchange programs with a college in the Bahamas? Does your school sponsor any study trips there? Is there a Caribbean Studies department on campus? Can you publish a paper about your experience in the Bahamas, or give a presentation to your peers when you return? The closer you can align your continuing education goals with the goals of the institution, the better your chances are for getting your trip approved and paid for.

In my experience, aligning my personal choices with institutional goals has been critical in getting approval and funding. One year, I was itching to use my professional development funds for a conference in France, but the library director said my request looked more like a vacation than professional development. I did some homework; a similar conference was scheduled in Mexico later that year. My institution was, at that time, starting to market itself to the growing pool of Mexican students who wanted to study in the U.S. Our administration was looking for ways to increase ties with Mexican academics. I put together a short proposal for my library director stating that attendance at this second conference would allow me to meet and begin forming relationships with Mexican academic librarians. The trip was approved; in fact, three more library staff members joined me. The conference was a success and became the catalyst for a long and beneficial relationship between our library staff and several librarians in Mexico.

Not all academic institutions pay for continuing education or can afford to cover all your expenses, but there are grants and scholarships available to help. Your library probably has reference books or databases listing grants. Several library associations sponsor conference travel grants or other professional development awards. The Mountain Plains Library Association, for example, sponsors a grants program that includes a travel grant for those who want to attend the annual meeting (www.usd.edu/mpla/grants.html). Check with your library association or search the American Library Association Web site, which lists several grants, awards, scholarships, fellowships, and exchanges for librarians who wish to attend conferences or pursue other opportunities:

- The American Library Association's list of American state and regional library associations (www.ala.org/ala/ ourassociation/chapters/stateandregional/ stateregional.htm)

- The American Library Association (www.ala.org)—use the search box on the home page for words such as "grant" or "award"

Continuing Education Plan: Your Institution's Policies

- What specific continuing education program, conference, etc. do you want to attend?

- Does it require travel? Or special equipment?

- How much does it cost? Include tuition fees, materials, online charges, travel expenses, hotel, and food, etc.

- Will this program fulfill your institution's continuing education policy?

- Will this program be covered by your institution's travel policy? In-state? Out-of-state? Out-of-country?

- How does this continuing education program match your orgnization's plan? Mission? Goals?

- What is the approval process? What paperwork do you need to complete in order to get your continuing education approved?

- Whose signatures do you need?

- What is the timeline for completing the paperwork?

Continuing Education Plan: Your Financial Resources

- How much money are you willing to contribute from your personal resources to continuing education?

- What continuing education funds are available to you from you institution?

  ◆ What are the rules for accessing those funds?

  ◆ What paperwork do you need to file?

  ◆ What are the deadlines?

- What continuing education funds are available from local/ regional organizations?

  ◆ What are the rules for accessing those funds?

  ◆ What paperwork do you need to file?

  ◆ What are the deadlines?

- What continuing education grants are available from national/ international organizations?

  ◆ What are the rules for accessing those funds?

  ◆ What paperwork do you need to file?

  ◆ What are the deadlines?

As you collect all this information, including Web site addresses, continuing education announcements, and official college forms, you should have a designated place to keep them together. The easiest method is to keep a folder in your desk to store all printouts, clippings, or forms related to your continuing education/professional development plan. This keeps you organized and on target.

Continuing Education Plan: Your Folder

Keep a continuing education/professional development folder in your desk. Review the contents at least once a year. Your folder should include the following items:

- Your current job description

- The job descriptions of any potential future positions, or of your "dream job"

- Your updated resume

- Your continuing education plan

- Your institution's mission, goals, and objectives and any special projects being undertaken

- The institution's mission, goals, and objectives and any special projects it is undertaking

- Copy of your institution's travel policies

- Copies of any continuing education/professional development announcements and applications forms

- Printouts from your favorite continuing education information Web sites, including the URLs

- Copies of any institutional continuing education/professional development approval, travel, or reimbursement forms

- A calendar with the dates of any interesting conferences, workshops, etc. circled; also dates of any applications, approval, or spending deadlines

- The name, phone number, and e-mail address of anyone whose help or signature you will need to get approval or funding

Carpe Diem

"Change will happen," Carol Ebbinghouse, Library Director at Western State University College of Law, reminds us. "Your library will be very different in a year or two, perhaps three months from now.

How different is up to you and your ability to learn, plan, implement, and sell the changes … you must become a change agent with a clear vision of the future (pp. 110, 113)." Whether you take a variety of one-day hands-on workshops to help you update specific job skills, or you decide to pursue a new degree, continuing education is the means by which you can achieve your personal and professional goals. A well-considered continuing education plan can serve as a guide for your development and career advancement. A good plan will also help you mesh your personal and professional goals with the mission and goals of your academic institution.

If you don't want the future to take you by surprise—seize the day, make a plan, and draw your own roadmap for tomorrow.

My sincerest thanks to Brooke Sheldon and all of those who shared with me their time and insight.

Works Cited

Ebbinghouse, Carol. "Would You Hire You?: Continuing Education for the Information Professional." *Searcher*, 10 (2002): 110–115.

Grealy, Deborah S. "Lifelong Learning for Librarians: A Strategic Competency for White-Water Navigation." *Colorado Libraries*, 26.2 (2000): 6–7.

Hamilton-Pennell, Christine. "Getting Ahead by Getting Online." *Library Journal*, 127.19 (2002): 32–35.

Markgren, Susanne. "Lifelong Learning in Librarianship: Classes and Beyond." *Info Career Trends*, 5.3 (2004). 8 pars. Available 30 June 2004: www.lisjobs.com/newsletter/archives/may04smarkgren.htm

Oklahoma Department of Libraries. Office of Library Development. *Oklahoma Program Approval Manual for Certification*, 1999. 9 pars. Available 7 Jul. 2004: www.odl.state.ok.us/servlibs/certprog/progdef.htm

CHAPTER 9

Unions in Academic Libraries

Tina Maragou Hovekamp

"The ultimate business of education is human freedom."
—Stephen K. Bailey (1916–1982)

The decline of union membership has been consistently documented since 1983, the first year for which comparable union data became available. In 2003, union membership among American workers declined to 12.9 percent, down from 20.1 percent in 1983, with the private sector being primarily responsible for this change ("Union membership," p. 2; United States Bureau of the Census, p. 431). Interestingly, union membership among workers in the public sector is more than four times higher than that among private sector employees, based on the latest Current Population Survey conducted by the Bureau of Census for the Bureau of Labor Statistics. It is worth noting that the group with the highest current unionization rate of 37.7 percent includes education, training, and library occupations (United States Department of Labor). Union membership is highest in the Middle Atlantic and Pacific regions and lowest in the Sunbelt states.

In academic unionized environments, most professional librarians are in the same bargaining unit with the rest of the faculty on their campus, the result of applying the "community of interest" principle in determining the composition of bargaining units. The National Labor Relations Board (NLRB), the administrative body that regulates union activity in the private sector, has been particularly influential in this issue, consistently ruling that librarians in private academic institutions be included in the same bargaining unit with faculty. Such decisions have had considerable impact on unit composition even in the public sector. In addition, the library profession itself has advocated this close association with teaching faculty in the hopes of advancing its own professional and financial status. In 1993 and again in 2001 the Association of College & Research Libraries (ACRL) endorsed the following guideline on collective bargaining: "The policy of the Association of College and Research Libraries is that academic librarians shall be included on the same basis as their faculty colleagues in units for collective bargaining. Such units shall be guided by the standards and guidelines of ACRL pertaining to faculty and academic status."

The inclusion of academic librarians in the same bargaining unit with faculty has not come without a price. Often cited is the librarians' minority status at the table of negotiations and the subsequent neglect of our own particular needs. Library professionals complain that they are frequently underrepresented and compromised during bargaining negotiations. Considering the sometimes significant differences in their job duties compared to other faculty, there is indeed a high risk that librarians' special interests may not get enough attention. To enjoy the benefits of union representation, direct involvement in union matters is a must for library professionals. As others in the library literature have previously and repeatedly admonished (Mika, p. 182; Wood, p. 15), librarians should take an active role and become visible within their bargaining units in order to make sure their concerns are addressed.

In 1980, the well-known Yeshiva case was the cause of additional speculation regarding librarians' bargaining position in institutions of higher education. Specifically, in a question of faculty representation at Yeshiva University, a private institution, the U.S. Supreme Court denied the faculty's right to bargain collectively. The reason given for this decision was that the faculty at that campus exercised so much authority that they could be considered managerial employees. The ruling of the Court stifled private sector faculty organizing for more than two decades and raised questions about the desirability of academic librarians identifying with college faculty. As Deanna Wood argues, many librarians with supervisory responsibilities may consider themselves managerial; however, even among this class of library professionals there is a significant lack of control over budgetary and personnel decision-making.

Unlike private colleges and universities, which fall under the jurisdiction of NLRB, union issues at public institutions are regulated by individual state labor laws. There are approximately thirty states in the country that provide statutory provisions for collective bargaining. In the rest of the states ("right-to-work" states), the lack of union protection for public employees has limited considerably the power to win union recognition. Because most working librarians are public employees, state legislation is consequently very important for libraries that may wish to unionize.

There are three major teacher unions in the country, which represent faculty and academic librarians: The American Federation of Teachers (AFT), the National Education Association (NEA), and the American Association of University Professors (AAUP). The AFT began as a labor union; both the NEA and the AAUP began as professional organizations. Local NEA and AAUP chapters began functioning as union organizations in the 1950's, but both organizations have maintained a strong professional orientation up to the present. The AAUP in particular has positioned itself as an advocate of academic and professional goals such as academic freedom and shared governance (Unger, p. 1065).

Development of Faculty and Academic Library Unions

Organized labor has not had an easy course in this country, often finding itself in conflict with unsympathetic governments and legal environments traditionally allied with business and industry rather than labor. It was not until 1935 that the National Labor Relations Act, also known as the Wagner Act, acknowledged the workers' right to join unions and provided protection against management reprisal. This legislation established the National Labor Relations Board (NLRB) to enforce workers' rights to unionize and to administer the application of the law during union elections and labor disputes. This federal legislation and NLRB jurisdiction apply only to the private sector. Changes at the federal level for public institutions did not occur until 1962, when President Kennedy's Executive Order 10988 recognized the right of federal employees to engage in collective bargaining. Although Kennedy's Executive Order did not extend to the state and local level, it was quite influential in a series of new laws rapidly introduced among different states. A number of states used Executive Order 10988 as a model to pass legislation allowing public employees to bargain collectively. Today, labor policies at the state level vary widely in their specific provisions, including the type of employees covered, the issues considered "permissible" for collective bargaining, and the specific practices allowed (such as strikes).

The 1960s brought a surge of union movement at a time when the number of public employees was also rising rapidly. Between 1951 and 1980, federal employment rose by 24 percent while state and local public employment rose by about 227 percent (Kearney and Carnevale, p, 17). By 1975, a third of public employees were unionized, making it the most substantial segment of organized labor (Redenius, p. 7). It was within this political and legislative framework, and concurrent with the growing success of teachers' unions, that faculty and librarian organizing gained momentum. It was within the same context that faculty and librarian unionism in public colleges and universities surpassed the slowing rate of union organizing among private educational institutions. In fact, by 1997 the National Center for the Study of Collective Bargaining in Higher Education and the Professions found that over 96 percent of union-represented faculty members were in the public sector (Euben and Hustoles).

The most recent statistics on union involvement among academic libraries were published in the 1980s. "According to a 1981 survey of ACRL personal members, approximately one-fourth of all college and university librarians were involved in collective bargaining at that time. The study found that 87.5 percent of academic librarians represented by unions were in the same bargaining unit with the rest of the faculty on their campus (Carmack and Olsgaard, p. 148). Another survey in 1985 found that almost half of the Association of Research Libraries membership had union contracts for at least some employees (librarians and/or library support staff). The AFT and AAUP were the main bargaining organizations representing most of the organized library employees. Since 1985 there has been limited study of unionization in libraries; one has to look for information on faculty organizing, because academic librarians are usually part of the same bargaining unit. Unpublished estimates of union membership in 2003 indicated that 17.5 percent of "postsecondary teachers" were union members (Di Natale). Two-year and community colleges are much more likely to be unionized than research institutions. Indeed, in 1997 the National Center for the Study of Collective Bargaining in Higher Education and the Professions found that 62.6 percent of full-time instructional staff was unionized at two-year institutions and 30.6 percent of full-time instructional staff was unionized at four-year institutions (Euben and Hustoles).

Reasons to Unionize

According to Deanna Wood, unions come to campuses at the employees' instigation and are rarely active in recruiting new members on their own. Wood argues that unions may be the last resort to deal with crises where employees and management are already polarized. Employees turn to unions to resolve dissatisfaction with important aspects of their job. During the first two decades of faculty organizing, wages, benefits, and job security were important reasons for collective bargaining. However, over time there has been a shift in attitudes about unionization on campuses. Although economic factors initially attracted faculty toward unionization, increasing concern over issues such as academic freedom, autonomy, tenure or advancement policies, and participation in institutional policymaking have since become the main reasons faculty turns to unions for help (DeCew, p. 17).

In 1998, full-time faculty at the nation's largest two-year college, Miami-Dade Community College, unionized as a result of turbulent relations with administration. The union, voted down three times before, gained the support of 70 percent of voting faculty. The "heavy-handed tactics of the president," high increases in adjunct faculty at the expense of full-time teaching appointments, tenure disputes, arbitrary personnel decisions, and authoritarian governance caused faculty at that campus to organize. As a union official put it humorously, "Sometimes the best union organizers are the college presidents themselves" ("Miami-Dade's ..., p. 2"). The context generating the drive to organize is similar in other institutions of higher education. In 2002 the AAUP was voted to represent the University of Akron faculty despite strong opposition from the administration. "We have sort of moved over time from what would be considered a collegial form of governance to a corporate structure," said one of the professors at the University. "We [are] treated as factory workers rather than professionals" ("Union in, Governance Out, p. A10").

Private colleges recently re-entered the union-organizing arena, challenging the landmark Yeshiva principle and disputing the reality of faculty's role in institutional governance and decision making. In 1992, after more than a decade of union lethargy among private institutions, Delaware Valley College, a private institution, won union certification for its faculty. The main reason for bringing the union to the campus was the faculty's limited input in the college decision-making process. By the time the union was voted in, problems at Delaware Valley College had reached a crisis level due to the governing board's disregard of faculty recommendations on a series of hiring, promotion, and tenure decisions ("NLRB May End ...," p. A14). Two other recent NLRB rulings, at the University of Great Falls in Montana and at Manhattan College in New York, confirm that faculty at private institutions do not always have "managerial power" as argued in the Yeshiva ruling.

Colleges and universities, especially in the private sector, are often described as big businesses with a corporate culture that clashes with traditional notions of shared governance and faculty autonomy (Willis, p. A11; Aronowitz, p. 11). It is clear that within such environments powerlessness and distrust are the primary causes for organizing, with economic factors being a secondary consideration. However, dissatisfaction alone is not enough to bring unions to campus. Unions are one option to deal with workplace problems collectively, and employees who turn to them must feel that collective bargaining is the best option they have to address their interests. It is true that not all involved will necessarily agree on the desirability of union representation. Employees may have differing, even opposing, views on the appropriateness of unionization, but in the end, the majority decides for the whole group.

Union Structure and the Bargaining Process

Unions vary widely in character from place to place. Their origin, size, personalities of their officers, and membership affect their governance, daily operations, dues, even their involvement in political or social activities (Sloane and Witney, p. 125). Organized labor in the U.S. mainly consists of the AFL-CIO federation, national unions, and local unions. The AFL-CIO, which functions as a lobbying organization on behalf of the union movement, represents half of the national unions in the country. The AFT, for instance, is an AFL-CIO union. The rest of the national unions, for example the NEA or AAUP, work independently. The role of the national union is to organize local chapters and negotiate collective bargaining agreements for the member local chapters. National officials negotiate contracts because they employ individuals with expertise and experience in negotiating collective bargaining agreements. The local union officials, on the other hand, administer the agreement, making sure that the provisions of the contract are met, although they usually also participate in negotiations.

A union organizing drive starts when employees are interested in representation by a labor organization. After the union campaign gets the initial support of the employees, a certification election is set. Through a secret ballot, employees determine whether they wish to have the union represent them. With the support of appropriate labor legislation, and if the union is certified, the relationship of employer and employee changes. Employees now have the legal right to negotiate over work-related issues. In states without "right-to-work" laws, unions tend to seek what is called an "agency shop," making it mandatory for all bargaining unit members to pay dues. The union is obligated to represent all employees, even those who may have voted against it. The union, regardless of individual preference, also represents subsequently hired employees.

Through collective bargaining, employees and managers agree on the basic terms and conditions of employment as well as procedures by which the parties resolve disputes over the interpretation and application of the bargaining contract. The life of a contract is normally three to four years, with each party starting preparations for a new negotiations cycle a year or so in advance.

Stress may be unavoidable during these negotiations. The process of bargaining has been described as a combination of: "(1) poker game, with the largest pots going to those who combine deception, bluff, and luck, or the ability to come up with a strong hand on the occasions on which they are challenged or 'seen' by the other side; (2) an exercise in power politics, with the relative strengths of the parties being decisive; ... (3) a debating society, marked by both rhetoric and name calling ... [and] (4) a 'rational process,' with both sides remaining completely flexible and willing to be persuaded only when all the facts have been dispassionately presented" (Sloane and Witney, p. 180). Whether a given negotiation is a combination of these four characteristics or whether some predominate depends on the climate, personalities involved, and financial situation within which the bargaining takes place (Sloane and Witney, p. 180). Both management and union usually start the process by bringing to the table positions or proposals that may seem extreme but are actually just starting points. Within the parameters of what each party decides are maximum acceptable concessions and minimum bargaining objectives, flexibility is a major factor for the successful agreement on a final contract. Typically, once management and union enter negotiations, they are legally bound to do so in good faith. The general tenets of "good faith bargaining" include that the parties abide by the following:

- Agree to meet at reasonable times.

- Negotiate in good faith and with an open mind on issues such as wages, hours, or other terms and employment conditions.

- Finalize agreements in a written contract (Allen and Keaveny, p. 290).

There are three categories of bargaining issues: mandatory, permissive, and prohibited. Mandatory issues are subjects employers must bargain over, including wages, hours of employment, overtime, grievance procedures, arbitration, layoff and recall, and the like. Permissive subjects are those that neither party is under obligation to negotiate, although they may be discussed at the bargaining table—these may include a variety of areas. Finally, prohibited subjects are considered illegal under the National Labor Relations Act or, in the public sector, under the state labor law. It is worth noting that prohibited subjects may significantly limit the scope of bargaining. For example, a 1993 Ohio law compelled state universities to increase their faculty's teaching load while prohibiting bargaining on faculty workload. Efforts of the union to challenge the constitutionality of this law failed both at the state and federal level. Similar examples in other states indicate that prohibited subjects may often be used to minimize union influence (Saltzman, p. 7).

Once negotiations start, they usually develop through three distinct stages. Discord and antagonism characterize the first stage as management and union try to identify their settlement range and the other party's resistance points. The second phase is different from the initial one, friendlier in tone, characterized by give-and-take discussions. Finally, the third stage, which concludes the negotiations, is usually the most intense and heated. During this stage the parties either reach an agreement or may face the threat of a strike (Allen and Keaveny, pp. 328–330).

The vast majority of negotiations end with a written contract, which the union brings to its constituents for voting and ratification. If the parties fail to reach an agreement, strike is a possible outcome;

however, this may be prohibited by a nonstrike clause included in agreements for the duration of a collective bargaining contract (although a union may strike after the expiration of the contract). In general, work stoppages are quite rare, especially in the public sector. Among higher education institutions between 1984–1994, there was a national total of only forty-eight strikes by faculty, with the majority of them taking place in the mid-1980s. The number of work stoppages since the 1980s has significantly tapered off (Rhoades, p. 15). For example, in 1998 there were 300 strikes in the private sector and only four in government. In much of the public sector, strikes are outlawed due to the "essential" nature of government services. In fact, in thirty-five states work stoppages are illegal for all or some public employees (Kearney and Carnevale, p. 224, 235). Within these settings, alternative mechanisms such as mediation, fact-finding, or arbitration may be available to deal with dispute resolution.

The "Collective" Outcomes of Unionization

The effects of unions on campuses differ from place to place. Given that librarians usually belong in the same bargaining unit with other faculty, they experience the same outcomes from their contractual agreements. Collective bargaining agreements may include specific clauses for librarians, but in general, the effects of unionization are shared with the rest of the campus. Some of the most important outcomes include effects on compensation, job security, governance, and general organizational climate, including academic freedom.

Because of the traditional view of unions as instrumental in improving financial or other "extrinsic" aspects of the employees' lives as well as the very fact that these extrinsic aspects are easier to measure, research has concentrated on the effects of unionization on salaries and working conditions. According to the U.S. Department of Labor, between 1975 and 1982 union pay rose much faster than nonunion pay across all industries. In contrast, between 1982 and 1999, nonunion pay rose faster. Despite these trends, union wages still tend to be higher even when they are not rising as rapidly as nonunion wages ("Union–Nonunion ..."). In academic institutions, unions tend to decrease discrepancies among faculty salaries and bring more salary parity, with those at the lower end of the pay scale benefiting the most. Evidence shows that the impact of unionism in two-year and four-year colleges is much more positive than in research university institutions. Labor economist Javed Ashraf studied the *National Study of Post-Secondary Faculty, 1993* and found that the union wage effect at public two-year colleges was 8.43 percent and only 2.83 percent in comprehensive universities (Ashraf, "Collective Bargaining," pp. 397–398). The same researcher found negative trends in unionized faculty wages among research and doctoral universities as compared to their nonunion counterparts (Ashraf, "Faculty Unionism," pp. 303–310). Ashraf attributed this phenomenon to a more equitable distribution of salary in union environments that do not favor "superstar" faculty, who tend to earn much more in nonunionized campuses. Another explanation offered was that unions improve the overall compensation package rather than just salary, often with "lower teaching loads, more generous terms for sabbatical leaves, higher summer compensation, higher levels of travel budgets for attendance at conferences, better retirement benefits, etc." (Ashraf, "Faculty Unionism," p. 308).

Salary increases in unionized campuses are usually determined by seniority. Unions do not generally favor merit pay, although there are contracts that include merit-based compensation increase clauses. According to Gary Rhoades, contractual provisions using the term *merit* are not very frequent, but occur most commonly among four-year institutions (pp. 37–40). Still, even when merit provisions are included, such pay increases are not as large as in nonunion environments (DeCew, pp. 57–58).

Job security is another major issue affected by collective bargaining agreements. Contractual language usually includes strong and specific clauses on tenure as well as due process and grievance procedures. Union advocates often point out that limited control over budgets and increasing reliance on part-time faculty positions or distance education technology are serious threats to faculty job security. Librarians experience the additional threat of being replaced by paraprofessional staff. Union contracts with strong emphases on tenure, due process, and grievance procedures make it procedurally and politically difficult to dismiss faculty. When layoffs are necessary, seniority and full-time status are often the main determinants, although as Gary Rhoades points out, management often has the discretion to fire even tenured faculty based on financial exigency or program realignments. Still, the likelihood of laying off tenured faculty in a unionized setting is quite limited, due to the accompanying costs and legal complexities (pp. 83–129). In addition to compensation and job security, union contracts often provide for sabbaticals, research support, and educational opportunities. Unionized academic professionals may also enjoy generous health benefits; maternity, paternity, or adoption leave; generous vacation and holidays; and tuition remission for employees and their dependents.

How does it really feel working in a unionized campus? Is it true that unions bring strain and conflict, or do they promote collegiality? Opposing views reflect how the effect of unions varies widely from place to place. The extent of collegial versus adversarial effects on each individual campus is very much influenced by the character of the union and the specific personalities involved at the negotiating table. Proponents of unions argue that unionization is instrumental in promoting a more collegial environment. By opening up communication, unions can help a campus that has experienced strain develop better working relations between faculty and administration. Unions can actually alleviate conflict by providing a forum to establish mutually agreed upon policies and procedures for decision-making. Opponents of unions argue the opposite. Their view is that the mere presence of unions implies adversarial relationships, strain, and conflict, all of which are incompatible with the ideals of academic life. Administrators in particular often argue that unions bring inflexibility and hinder the process of efficient and effective decision-making through institution of complex and bureaucratic contractual procedures.

Regardless of these arguments, it is hard to deny that unionization provides a venue to secure the employees' role in college governance. The effect of unions in academia seems particularly strong in environments that had previously experienced problems with shared governance. Within these environments, unions are usually able to address both issues of empowerment and traditional "bread-and-butter" issues (Castro, p. 48). Collective bargaining guarantees the employees representation in the shaping of their working conditions. However, critics argue that the union model may actually remove faculty from a more active and immediate role in campus governance. According to Judith DeCew, "On issues such as conditions of appointment and educational policy, traditionally decided by faculty senates or committees reporting to the senate, unions often take over the decisions or negotiations" (p. 65). It is important to remember that unions are advocates for faculty interests, playing a role that in nonunionized environments may easily be lacking or ineffective.

As part of their general advocacy for their membership, unions also exert significant influence on the issue of academic freedom. Unions are strong advocates of freedom of speech and provide formal protections of employees' rights to express themselves. The AAUP in particular has a strong tradition of support for academic freedom, something that librarians are tuned in to through their professional training. Union contracts explicitly secure employees' rights to speak openly about their views, regardless of how unpopular. These contractual protections are extremely important, considered among the most essential clauses in negotiating agreements (Wood, p. 14). Although academic freedom may be presented as a working principle around unionized campuses, it may lack the formal and binding backing that a contractual agreement provides.

Conclusion

Unions may affect the workplace in very significant ways. If you are considering entering a unionized environment, find out more about the following:

1. The impact of union presence on bread-and-butter issues such as compensation, working conditions, and benefits including sabbatical leaves and continuing education

2. Specific agreements related to job security for the employees including union support for due process and grievance procedures on behalf of the employees

3. Agreed upon contractual provisions for promotion and salary increases

4. The role of the union in campus governance, including a definition of permissible and prohibited subjects for negotiations

5. The overall effectiveness of the union in representing the interests of the whole membership and the extent of union commitment on the part of its membership

6. The organizational climate as reflected in the nature of the relationship between union and administration

7. How the library fits into the union and how satisfied librarians are with their representation

If you are contemplating working in a union environment, take the time to understand how it works and how it can benefit you. Learn about the history of unionization on the campus and find out what people think of the situation. As with other career issues, the better your understanding going in, the better your odds of success.

Works Cited

Allen, Robert E., and Keaveny, Timothy J. *Contemporary Labor Relations.* 2nd ed. Reading, MA: Addison-Wesley, 1998.

Aronowitz, Stanley. *The Knowledge Factory: Dismantling the Corporate University and Creating True Higher Education.* Boston: Beacon Press, 2000.

Ashraf, Javed. "Faculty Unionism in the 1990s: A Comparison of Public and Private Universities." *Journal of Collective Negotiations,* 28 (1999): 303–310.

———. "Collective Bargaining and Compensation at Public Junior Colleges." *Journal of Collective Negotiations in the Public Sector,* 27 (1998): 393–399.

Association of College & Research Libraries. *Guideline on Collective Bargaining.* Available 11 May 2004: www.ala.org/ala/acrl/acrlstandards/guidelinecollective.htm

Association of Research Libraries, Office of Management Studies. *Unionization in ARL Libraries.* Flyer no. 118. Washington, D.C.: Systems and Procedures Exchange Center, 1985.

Carmack, Bob, and John N. Olsgaard. "Collective Bargaining among Academic Librarians: A Survey of ACRL Members." *College & Research Libraries,* 43 (1982): 140–148.

Castro, Consuelo Rey. "Community college faculty satisfaction and the faculty union." *New Directions for Institutional Research,* 105 (2000): 45–55.

DeCew, Judith Wagner. *Unionization in the Academy.* Lanham, MD: Rowman & Littlefield Publishers, 2003.

Di Natale, Marisa. "Re: Union Statistics." E-mail to author. 11 May 2004.

Euben, Donna, and Thomas P. Hustoles. *Collective Bargaining: Revised and Revisited.* Mar 2003. Available 14 May 2004: www.aaup.org/Legal/info%20outlines/legcb.htm

Kearney, Richard C., and David G. Carnevale. *Labor Relations in the Public Sector.* 3rd ed. New York: Marcel Dekker, 2001.

Mass, Michael A., and Anita F. Gottlied. "Federally Legislated Collective Bargaining for State and Local Government." *Labor Relations in the Public*

Sector: Readings and Cases. 2nd ed. Ed. Marvin J. Levine. (pp. 76–87). Columbus, OH: Publishing Horizons, 1985.

"Miami-Dade's Faculty Hand Union a 'Huge Win' in Florida." *Community College Week*, 6 April 1998: 2.

Mika, Joseph J. "Collective Bargaining: Still a Relevant Issue." *Catholic Library World*, 57 (1986): 181–182.

"NLRB May End Its Opposition to Unions for Private-College Professors." *Chronicle of Higher Education*, 9 Jan 1998: A14.

Redenius, Charles. "Public Employees: Survey of Some Critical Problems on the Frontier of Collective Bargaining." *Labor Relations in the Public Sector: Readings and Cases.* 2nd ed. Ed. Marvin J. Levine. (pp. 7–22). Columbus, OH: Publishing Horizons, 1985.

Rhoades, Gary. *Managed Professionals: Unionized Faculty and Restructuring Academic Labor.* Albany, N.Y: State University of New York Press, 1998.

"Salt Lake Faculty Unionize—Two Other Utah Colleges on the Verge." *Community College Week*, 29 June 1998: 10.

Saltzman, Gregory M. "Higher Education Collective Bargaining and the Law." *The NEA 2001 Almanac of Higher Education.* 2001. Available 10 May 2004: www.nea.org/he/healma2k1/a01p45.pdf

Sloane, Arthur A., and Fred Witney. *Labor relations.* 10th ed. Upper Saddle River, NJ: Prentice Hall, 2001.

Unger, Harlow G. "Teacher Unions." *Encyclopedia of American Education.* 2nd ed. New York: Facts on File, 2001.

"Union In, Governance Out." *Chronicle of Higher Education*, 10 October 2003: p. A10.

"Union Membership 2003." *Monthly Labor Review*, Feb. 2004: 2.

"Union–Nonunion Wage Gap Narrows." *Monthly Labor Review*, 25 April 2000. Available 25 May 2004: www.bls.gov/opub/ted/2000/apr/wk4/art02.htm

United States Bureau of the Census. *Statistical Abstracts of the United States.* Washington, DC: GPO, 2003.

United States Department of Labor. *Union Membership (Annual)*, 21 Jan 2004. Available 6 May 2004: www.bls.gov/news.release/union2.toc.htm

Willis, Ellen. "Why Professors Turn to Organized Labor." *New York Times*, 28 May 2001: A11.

Wood, Deanna. "Librarians and Unions: Defining and Protecting Professional Values." *Education Libraries*, 23.1(1999): 12–16.

CHAPTER 10

What Have You Been Up To?— Documenting Your Career

McKinley Sielaff

"There is the necessity of bringing results to light in the form of publication, for in the academic scheme of things results unpublished are little better than those never achieved."
—Logan Wilson (1907–1990)

What feelings do the terms tenure, promotion, and evaluation evoke for you? They may sound like stressful times on the job. Doubtless, you will experience evaluations on your job. Tenure, reappointment tests, whatever they may be called, evaluation by any other name is still evaluation. When done well, evaluations can be a rewarding experience and a wonderful tool to help gauge progress and career development. Done poorly, they can elicit anxiety, apprehension, and frustration. This part of our jobs will always create stress but with some preparation and foresight, perhaps we can cut down our level of concern.

The dossier, or tenure document, is an extensive written record of your professional accomplishments. It includes documentation of publications, training, professional association activities, presentations, and more. It may fill several ring binders or boxes. As a librarian with faculty status, you will normally be required to compile a dossier and submit it for review on a regular basis. However, there are other scenarios where having a current vita (documents beyond and more inclusive than a current resume) can come in very handy. You may be writing a grant proposal, filling out an application, or seeking a certification. You may accept a tenure track job in the future or want to advance beyond your current status. A dossier helps you gain an understanding of the different responsibilities and roles you have participated in during your career. Many of the individual aspects included in the dossier, such as service or research, are covered in detail in separate chapters of this book.

Documenting your education and experience provides a framework with which to view your entire work history. Used as a career map, a dossier shows us where we are, then points out directions where we can go—plotting the next steps for training, education, and career development. Such a map illuminates your strengths and weaknesses. Consequently, it can also inform you about your appeal by matching expertise with skills sought in job ads. A well-documented dossier can also highlight your worthiness for merit pay or promotion.

There are personal rewards too. Upon earning tenure, I felt a genuine sense of accomplishment. I saw the contributions I had made to the profession through my pursuit of tenure as well as the professional growth and development I had gained. Even while currently working at a college without faculty status for librarians, I have a deeper and better understanding of what the process is like for faculty colleagues on campus. Judy Fletcher adds another point: When you are stuck in your career, a dossier is a positive reminder of the work you have accomplished (Reese, pp. 18–21). Whatever the reason may be, documenting your professional life from the beginning will help you as you move forward in your career. Whether it is to delineate professional growth, outline reasons for promotion or a raise, or provide a listing of accomplishments, recording your work is important.

Preliminary Questions and the Timeframe

Given the importance of the review and tenure process, it is critical to find out about it in advance. During an interview, you will most likely be asked about your research interests. You may want to inquire about what types of scholarship library faculty members are engaged in. William Vincenti, Reference Librarian and 2004 tenure candidate at Montclair State University, suggests "ask about the winds of change regarding the tenure and evaluation process including any proposed or planned changes that may be initiated in the near future." Finding out about scheduled performance reviews during an interview is a great idea, but do not stop there. Once employed, seek further clarity regarding what the expectations are to enable you to succeed and excel. The requirements should be stated in a formal document. You should keep the requirements of your institution in mind as you create your dossier. If there is an evaluation form, scrutinize it.

"You should also be mindful of other informal (unwritten and unspoken) values," according to David Thomas, Professor at Harvard Business School (Thompson, pp. 88–90). Talk with colleagues. Talk with your supervisor. Asking for clarification is one way to avoid a bad review or worse. Try to determine the organization's perceptions and biases. For example, how much time should you spend on scholarship? Are you allowed time during the workweek to pursue research, and if so, how much? How many, what type, and where should you give presentations? Is presenting a paper at one conference more prestigious than at a different one? How important is it where you publish? Does inclusion in certain journals "count" more than others? Some suggest "librarians in all universities should take care to inquire closely about the criteria used to judge publications in their particular institutions" (Bradigan and Mularski, pp. 360–366). Will individual work be more valued, and thus rated more highly, than work done with another or others? Are professional memberships important? If so, which ones, and should you be volunteering your services to any?

Your dossier represents years of work. It will take you time to advance through the tenure system. First, you need to establish your reappointment timetable. Find out how often you will be reviewed; it may not be every year. Learn to look at your reviews in a positive light. They are an important stage in the promotion and tenure process. During the reviews you must confirm that you are indeed meeting (or even exceeding) the established measures for reappointment as well as following tenure criteria.

What happens if you are not performing up to standard? How will a bad review in any given year affect the overall outcome? What can you do to overcome or make up for negative reviews? Can you be terminated before the tenure year if you are not making sufficient progress toward tenure? Conversely, if you are performing well, can you expedite the process? If so, do requirements differ for an early review than for the regular process? Expectations may change for candidates applying early. Do you need more publications, presentations, service, awards, and so forth for early tenure? How frequently have colleagues pursued early tenure? How often have they been successful? Find out what happens after you turn in your dossier and after a tenure decision is made. If successful, are there further reviews, is promotion built-in to the tenure process, and are there financial benefits? Ascertain what happens to unsuccessful candidates. What is the review policy following a denial? Will you need to supply further materials?

These answers are critical; the responses to these questions will affect how and what you do between reviews. A clear understanding of evaluation criteria, your job's objectives, and how performance is measured is important so that evaluations do not come as a surprise (Thompson, pp. 88–90). A reappointment dossier speaks on your behalf; it is usually your responsibility to provide a reappointment committee with the necessary information and documentation to establish that you have met the criteria for reappointment. In all likelihood, you will not have the opportunity to speak in person with those evaluating your dossier. They may not know you; all they have to go on are the written words and documents before them.

Areas for Evaluation of Tenure

- Professional responsibility

- Teaching effectiveness

- Research and creative activities

- Service activities

- Directed professional activities

- Administrative duties

You become an effective librarian through progressive development of expertise, achievements, experience, increasing responsibilities, and contributing to the overall work of the library. Accordingly, you are assessed on specific aspects of your job. You may be required to rate your specific skills such as judgment, knowledge and quality of work, communication, cooperation, responsibility, self-improvement/professional development, supervisory skills, initiative, problem solving, and so on. You may need to address your job responsibilities, administrative and managerial skills, presentation of instruction, scholarly activities, professional activities, and other contributions to your institution and the scholarly communities. A reappointment dossier typically contains a personal statement on why reappointment is merited, a current curriculum vitae, evidence of job performance and scholarship, copies of publications, notification of awards and honors received, and other supporting documentation and required forms as well as all prior performance evaluations. David Kruger, Reference Librarian and 2003 tenure recipient at the University of Wyoming, comments "potential only goes so far. There needs to be a solid plan of action articulated throughout."

Documentation Outcomes of Each Dossier Section

For each section think in terms of:
1. A description including a
   a. Summary of responsibilities
   b. Analyses of work accomplished
2. Documentation of the outcomes
3. Evaluation
4. Signs of prominence and distinction
5. Self-reflective appraisal

Teaching

The scope of teaching for academic librarians is more varied and broader in scope than classroom instruction. Library-related teaching may include working with patrons, preparing for job assignments, communicating with staff, and staying current with trends in the necessary fields of expertise. A successful dossier demonstrates a command of the subject matter, knowledge of resources and tools used in the performance of responsibilities, and a grasp of general and specific objectives. An effective librarian is one who advances library service and access to resources by:

- Facilitating and participating in outreach efforts

- Engaging in and organizing an area of service for the accomplishment of program objectives

- Planning, organizing, and coordinating library services, facilities, and resources

- Matching course curriculum and programs with library services and resources

- Coaching users in research methodologies necessary for life-long learning

- Raising awareness of the relationship between one subject to other fields of knowledge

- Encouraging users to develop library skills for independent use of library resources through reference service and library user aids

- Demonstrating superior communication and presentation skills

- Strengthening library resources and research collections

- Developing and using bibliographic and information systems in order to facilitate access to information

- Interpreting library resources to patrons through reference service or through preparation of catalogs, guides, or bibliographies

- Constructing networks to make resources available to users

- Showing interest and enthusiasm for teaching and learning

Think about the activities you have performed related to teaching. Provide descriptions of your work such as a summary of responsibilities and activities along with copies of materials developed to enhance instruction (policies, reports, procedures, manuals, proposals, guidelines, handouts, bibliographies, finding aids, and training materials). Include examples of electronic/virtual materials. These additional documents also support teaching outcomes:

- User satisfaction surveys and user/usage statistics

- Self-study reports for outside accrediting agencies and academic program reviews

- Comparisons of resources to those of peer institutions and collection evaluation measures

- Evidence of enhanced access to materials and resources

- Evidence of enhanced organization of materials

- Grant and contract proposals developed and submitted to funding agencies

Another group of materials to include are observations of your effectiveness and contributions from students, administrators, colleagues, and your supervisor; comments regarding accreditation reviews in which you have participated; recognition from campus or professional associations or other outside agencies; invitations to teach, lecture, or present workshops; and other relevant awards or commendations.

Scholarship

Standards of scholarship are based on understanding and contributing to the field of librarianship and your area(s) of specialization. You can make significant scholarly contributions through a variety of activities and publications. Your dossier should demonstrate creative and analytical abilities in developing, evaluating, and documenting library programs, systems, and procedures. Scholarly and artistic endeavor could include development of bibliographical tools, scholarly and creative work, involvement in basic and applied research, exhibitions, writing and publication, and presentations to professional and learned societies. The scope of research and creative activity is quite broad. To document the effectiveness of your scholarship, include in your dossier descriptions summarizing and analyzing the work along with examples of your results (e.g., articles). External evaluations should also be included. These may be from colleagues on your campus as well as other institutions and students, department/division heads, curators, critics, reviewers, or other independent experts.

Service

To organize your service activities, think of service in terms of the beneficiaries such as service to one's institution (outside the library), service to the discipline, and service to external communities. You should participate in institutional affairs through service and leadership in your area(s) of expertise. You might provide leadership in or make significant contributions to campus committees or groups, develop and revise policy documents, participate in campus governance, mentor others (employees or student groups), or partner with other departments to develop programs. Another kind of service includes activities that enhance your institution's effectiveness such as designing and directing faculty development activities, providing specialized research or information services for the campus or community, or planning and directing formal outreach programs.

However, service should extend past campus boundaries. Service to the discipline may result in holding a leadership position in an organization, organizing workshops for professional groups, serving on accreditation bodies, serving on the editorial board of a professional journal, reviewing articles and books, or participating on committees of professional organizations. Services to external communities might mean conducting contracted research; consulting and providing technical assistance to public and private organizations; informing general audiences through seminars, conferences, and lectures; interpreting technical information for a variety of audiences; testifying before the legislature and Congressional committees; serving as an expert for the press and other media; or collaborating with schools, other libraries, and civic organizations.

Along with a summary of your service responsibilities and activities, analyze your accomplishments. Include examples such as:

- The number of people you served and who benefited from your service

- Official documents and reports resulting from an activity

- Illustrations of ways in which the activity enhanced the overall group

- Published articles, technical reports, or monographs

- Grant proposals

- Log of activities, e.g., programs presented

- Visibility of the activity

Assessments and letters from the beneficiaries of your service belong in your dossier, as do evaluations from sponsoring organizations, colleagues and other peers, honors and awards recognizing service, and election or appointment as officer in professional organizations.

Other Professional Activity

Professional development is important because it leads to growth in expertise and enhanced service. Activities in this category include continued educational development through advanced study and participation in short courses, seminars, workshops, internships, special conferences, and the like, together with involvement and participation in associations. Documentation for professional activity might include a written description of the scope of the project and participation and analyses of the work accomplished. Include assessments of your activity such as evaluations by peers, participants, administrators, and other constituents. Record new programs and initiatives resulting from these activities. As well as mentioning honors and awards, state the degree to which the activity brings positive visibility to your institution, grants received, and contracts negotiated.

Administration may not be an essential component of your job. Nevertheless, you need to demonstrate leadership and organizational skills in planning, developing, and coordinating library activities and programs. This is accomplished through exercising initiative to advance library services, interpreting policies and procedures accurately, coordinating functions of one work area with other areas of the library, and working collegially to accomplish the goals and objectives of library programs. You should also exhibit expertise in motivating and guiding the work of others, in delegating authority and responsibility, and in judiciously evaluating personnel. Leadership tasks—such as heading a department/division, directing special projects, and participating in special task forces, commissions, and self-studies—are significant contributions to your institution and, rightly, are often separated out for distinction. Means of demonstrating these measures include:

- Recruiting, selecting, training, and supervising staff
- Budgeting (planning, requesting, and allocating funds for the library)
- Identifying problems and offering compelling solutions
- Setting objectives and planning their execution
- Showing effectiveness in decision making and execution of policy decisions
- Encouraging outstanding performance
- Treating staff impartially and being sensitive to their needs
- Establishing effective training programs
- Communicating effectively with administrators, colleagues, and staff
- Keeping aware of new methods and technological changes
- Serving on administrative committees

For each series of the criteria required in your reappointment dossier (teaching, research, service, etc.) conduct a self-appraisal. It should reflect your responsibilities, show evidence of steps you have taken to improve your performance, professional development and achievements, and list further career goals. Consider keeping a journal or log as a concise way to underscore and highlight your work.

Documented Outcomes

For Teaching
- Teaching materials
- Invitations to teach, lecture, and present workshops
- Self-study reports submitted for outside accrediting agencies and academic program reviews
- User satisfaction surveys and user/usage statistics
- Class/instruction assessments

- Statement about your teaching
- Comparisons of library resources to those of peer institutions and collection evaluation measures
- Evidence of enhanced access to materials and resources
- Evidence of enhanced organization of materials

For Scholarship
- Descriptions of the research or creative activity by summarizing and analyzing the work
- Publications (journal articles, books, book chapters, edited books, monographs, translations, abstracts, and reviews)
- Indexes, union lists, finding lists, pathfinders, Webographies, thesauri, catalogs, and bibliographies
- Technical and training material
- Electronic publishing
- Computer programs
- Web pages and Internet sites
- Papers presented at professional meetings
- Displays, art shows, performances, and exhibits

Of Service
- Letters or e-mails of acknowledgment of your service acitivities
- Illustrations of ways in which the activity enhanced your institution
- Representing your institutional needs to vendors
- Honors, awards, and acknowledgments conferred
- Number of people served and benefited
- Official documents and reports resulting from an activity
- Leadership in an organization
- Serving as an editor
- Organizing workshops and conferences
- Serving on accreditation bodies
- Conference program showing committee work, panel participation, and facilitating work
- Committee work—reports and publications
- Committee minutes outlining your active role
- Published articles, technical reports, or monographs

- Newspaper or magazine articles describing service, project, or display
- Log activities, e.g., programs presented
- Outcomes of mentoring others
- Visibility of the activity

Additional Professional Activity
- Educational development through short courses, seminars, workshops, internships, etc.
- Written description of project and level of participation
- Administrative duties:
  - Supervising staff
  - Establishing effective training programs
  - Budgeting: planning, requesting, and allocating funds
  - Identifying problems and problem-solving solutions
  - Showing effective decision making and execution of decisions
  - Communicating effectively with other administrators and campus employees
- Implementing new methods and technological advances
- Grants applied for and/or obtained, award letters, and other external funding
- Log of activities, e.g., programs presented
- Visibility of the activity
- Awards and scholarships, honors received including photographs of plaques or nonpaper awards
- External statements regarding evaluations of your activities

Getting It Together

Use your resume as the official record of what you have already accomplished. Keep it up-to-date with professional work history and education, specialized training, and language skills. Keep lists of publications, presentations, research and grant activities, awards, scholarships, and volunteer and personal interests. Keep an original copy of each item. Collect materials and document your progress as you go, continuously building and saving potential dossier inclusions. Write up periodic (weekly or monthly) summaries of what you have accomplished and completed, to help remember your work. Use these notes as you begin documenting for your annual review. Err on the side of excess and save anything even remotely possible to put in a dossier; do not overlook personal life experience that has a bearing on your work. You can cull through materials come reappointment time. Planning and collecting along the way helps avoid being overwhelmed and under-prepared later.

Use work from your daily activities to build your dossier. Think about what further use you can find for a handout you have already created for a class. Maybe there is a clearinghouse for such materials, or it could be reworked as a Webliography. Perhaps there are colleagues at other institutions who could use it, or it could serve as a basis for in-house training or as a conference presentation or poster. Start with small projects and build up. Collaborate on projects with others to share the demands that come with research. Volunteering your services is another way to ease into scholarship. Besides fulfilling service requirements, it bestows name recognition, which can often lead to future opportunities to serve on committees and work on projects.

Previews and Run-Throughs

First, cover the basics. Make sure there are no typos and no spelling or grammatical errors in your dossier and associated documents. Follow any formatting standards outlined in the rules and regulations. Make sure there are no omissions; match listed documents in your resume to the appropriate place in your dossier. Review the dossiers of others; you may want to model yours on those of colleagues who have proven successful. Analyze what is good about them, what is included, and what is confusing or ambiguous. Revise your dossier as needed.

Be proactive in asking others to help you through the entire process. Take advantage of formal mentoring programs either in your own library or through a library association. Michelle Mach offers this counsel "often the wisest and most honest advice I received was from nontenured librarians who were two or three years ahead of me on the tenure track. Because they were going through the process themselves, their advice tended to be direct and to the point" (Shontz, p. 122). After all, most tenure processes have a peer evaluation component so getting a jump on what your peers think of your dossier is good practice.

Learn from each review. Build on the strengths pointed out during the review and correct the weak spots. With any sort of evaluation—a glowing review or a thumb's down—ask for clarification on points you do not understand. Inquire why you did well or why you received below average or poor ratings. Most importantly, ask what you can do to improve.

Tips for the Tenure/Evaluation Process

- Ask about scheduled performance reviews

- Find mentor(s) and talk with others about tenure

- Know your timeline

- Jot down tasks on a frequent and regular basis

- Keep resume up to date

- Use resume as a reminder of things for your dossier

- Keep documents all together (from kudos to completed evaluation forms)

- Balance all aspects of all criteria: teaching, scholarship, service, etc.

- Balance types of evidence (journal articles and in-house guides, etc.)

- Have a visible reminder of your goals and review it

- Follow specified formatting standards

- Get your dossier reviewed prior to turning it in

Conclusion

Your job description lists basic responsibilities and duties that you must fulfill. Beyond that, there are expectations of what you should be spending time doing. You will be evaluated on how well you accomplish these additional tasks. Focus on all your tasks when composing an annual review or pulling together a dossier. You were hired because you showed promise as an academic librarian. To advance, you must display additional characteristics; this is the very nature of tenure. Accordingly, the criteria used to assess your effectiveness are designed to reflect increasing capability and professional growth.

Create a picture for yourself of what the process is all about by reading the regulations on tenure for librarians, talking with colleagues, and viewing their dossiers so you can gain a better understanding of what is required of you and demystify the tenure process. Next, create a plan of action. Create a time line of how much work you need to do by a certain point and the time it will take. Give yourself plenty of time—no one can create a professional career in a week. Keep a running account of all you do and retain copies of your work as well as comments about it. Find mentors who will let you examine their dossiers and comment on yours.

The first years as a librarian can be overwhelming as you accumulate knowledge and experience in the workplace. These years are the foundation of your career. Your dossier is all about taking credit for the work you have done and the successes you have achieved. By starting right, you will be managing a successful and satisfying career.

Works Cited

Bradigan, Pamela S., and Carol A. Mularski. "Evaluation of Academic Librarians' Publications for Tenure and Initial Promotion." *Journal of Academic Librarianship*, 22 (1996): 360–366.

"Guidelines for Academic Status for College and University Librarians." American Library Association. 2003. Available 19 July 2004: www.ala.org/ala/acrl/acrlstandards/guidelinesacademic.htm

Reese, Susan. "Teaching Portfolios: Displaying the Art of Teaching." *Techniques: Connecting Education and Careers*, 79.5 (2004): 18–21.

Shontz, Priscilla. *Jump Start Your Career in Library and Information Science*. Lanham, MD: Scarecrow Press, 2002

Thompson, Carla. "How's Your Performance." *Black Enterprise*, 34.11 (2004): 88–90.

Vesper, Virginia, and Gloria Kelley. *Criteria for Promotion and Tenure for Academic Librarians*. Chicago: College Libraries Section, ACRL, 1997.

CHAPTER 11

Up North—Comparisons and Contrasts of U.S. and Canadian Academic Libraries

Don Taylor

"I accept now with equanimity the question so constantly addressed to me, 'Are you an American?' and merely return the accurate answer, 'Yes, I am a Canadian.'"
—Lester B. Pearson (1897–1972)

As is often the case in respect to distinctions between Canada and the United States, the casual observer might assume that the academic libraries of the two nations are indistinguishable. As an academic librarian who has worked in both countries, I am aware of how different the two systems can be. These differences stem from variations in the university systems, culture, and laws between the two nations. As a fellow Canadian who recently returned from working in a U.S. library told me, "Things can be so different despite so many surface similarities."

The Canadian University System

In Canada, all but a handful of post-secondary institutions (colleges and universities) are publicly funded. There are only 64 universities in Canada, with an additional thirty to forty university colleges and institutes that offer both bachelor degrees and two-year diploma degrees. Like the U.S., Canada has community colleges and technical institutes with two-year diploma programs, but unlike the U.S., Canada has no tradition of the four-year liberal arts college. Canada, with a population of 31 million, has significantly fewer universities per capita than the U.S. For example, the province of Manitoba (pop.

141

Comparisons of U.S. and Canadian Academic Libraries

	Canada	United States
Population	30 million	290 million
Post secondary institutions	300 approx[1]	4000 approx[2]
Universities	64[1]	1518[2]
Library schools	7	50 (includes Puerto Rico)
Library employment prospects	moderate[3]	good–v. good[4]
Librarian positions total	10,000[5]	167,000[6]

1 Association of Universities and Colleges of Canada and Canadian Association of University Teachers
2 U.S. Dept. of Education
3 Future of Heritage Work in Canada
4 ALA Recruitment and Retirement Survey (2001)
5 Approximate calculation from Statistics Canada data
6 Bureau of Labor Statistics

1.16 million) has three post-secondary institutions offering bachelor's degrees. In contrast, the neighbouring state of North Dakota (pop. 643,000) has eight post-secondary institutions offering bachelor's degrees.

One result of the greater per capita number of universities in the U.S. is a larger prestige gap among universities in the U.S. than exists among universities in Canada. The public funding of universities in Canada creates economies of scale where it is considered more efficient to spend money to grow existing universities and thus bring down the average cost per student. Five universities of 15,000 students each do not require the same number of services and faculty as fifteen universities of 5,000 students each. Canadian universities are located in larger urban areas and not in smaller locales around the provinces, thus leading to fewer universities being built and the absence of the "university town" from the Canadian landscape.

Education is strictly a provincial jurisdiction. Therefore, Canada has no federal department of education, nor are there national educational standards regarding curriculum. Provinces can become so protective of their turf that when the federal government introduced the new Millennium Scholarships for university students, some provinces complained that the scholarships were an intrusion into provincial jurisdiction and should not be allowed. Federal money flows into Canadian universities through general transfer payments to the provinces and through research funding agencies such as the National Research Council. However, in no way can the federal government earmark specific money for educational spending by the provinces.

Two other differences between Canadian and U.S. universities are the terminology and ranking differences between certain academic degrees. An important terminology difference is the use of "faculty" in place of "college" at Canadian universities. For example, in Canada it is called the Faculty of Arts instead of the College of Arts, the Faculty of Education instead of the College of Education. Canadian universities also treat professional degrees as bachelor's degrees. For example, in law, the J.D. in the U.S. is called the LL.B. in Canada and given the ranking of a bachelor's degree. At many U.S. universities, the teacher education programs are master's programs, but in Canada, those same programs are bachelor's programs, although the entry requirements may be the same. Because of this difference in degree rank, Canadian university libraries regard some post-baccalaureate professional degrees not as second bachelor's degrees, but more akin to a master's degree.

The Canadian University Library

Canadian universities have a single library system on campus. Consequently the medical or law library will always be part of the university library system and report to the university library director. Because they fall under the policies of the university-wide library system, public access to the medical and legal libraries on Canadian university campuses is usually less restrictive than that of U.S. law and medical libraries.

The university librarian in Canada does not have the title of dean but is instead called a director. Title notwithstanding, the director will often be on the university dean's committee. Aside from the largest research universities, there is no pressure for Canadian academic library directors to hold a Ph.D., which stems partly from the fact that Canadian university libraries are not academic departments.

The broader Canadian university community sees the academic library as a vital service. Librarians are often in a separate faculty group from the teaching and research faculty and do not usually hold the traditional faculty ranks of associate professor, assistant professor, and professor. They do not generally have as rigorous a tenure and review process as U.S. librarians with faculty status do. The Canadian university community sees academic librarians as valuable support for professors in their research and teaching needs, but not as active, or competitive, researchers. The sabbaticals and grant opportunities available to some U.S. faculty librarians are not as easily available to their Canadian counterparts.

The Canadian library world is small, resulting in the need to look outside of Canada for standards and for many new ideas and trends. Canadian academic libraries are heavily influenced by international practices, particularly from the United States. Canadian academic libraries use most of the same standards, such as Library of Congress Subject Headings. The U.S. spellings in LCSH cause problems for Canadian patrons, and it is not uncommon to have people ask at the reference desk why there are no books in the library on "labour unions" or "watercolour painting." In conjunction with LCSH, Canadian academic libraries also use Canadian Subject Headings (CSH), developed by Library and Archives Canada to reflect "Canadian cultural, economic, historical, literary, political, and social experience" (*Canadian Subject Headings*). For example, CSH uses the all-encompassing term Native peoples—Canada to represent Inuit, First Nations (Indians), and Metis. CSH is also used where there are differences between U.S. and Canadian terminology, such as Cabinet ministers in Canada versus Cabinet secretaries in the U.S.

Becoming a Librarian in Canada

Canadian academic libraries require a master's degree from an American Library Association (ALA) accredited library school. All seven library schools in Canada are ALA accredited. The accrediting team for Canadian library schools includes faculty from a Canadian library school and others with an understanding of Canadian universities and libraries. Six of the library schools are English language and one is French. The six English programs are at the University of British Columbia, University of Alberta, University of Western Ontario, University of Toronto, McGill University, and Dalhousie University; the French program is at Université de Montréal. Unique in North America, Québec has a licensing agency called the

Corporation des Bibliothécaires Professionels du Québec/Corporation of Professional Librarians of Québec (CORPU), which has the sole legal authority to enable a practitioner in Québec to use the title "Professional Librarian." The two library schools in Québec, McGill and Université de Montréal, work in close association with CORPU to ensure that their graduates are able to meet these standards.

The Job Market for Academic Librarians in Canada

Throughout the 1990s, the Canadian job market was bleak for librarians, with the number of librarian jobs shrinking 30 percent between 1992 and 2002 (Durand, p. 7). Currently things are looking up as Canadian demographics show an aging librarian population and an accompanying need for increased hiring over the next few years (Future of Heritage Work in Canada, p. 50), which bodes well for new graduates after the previous lean years. The retirement bubble forecast over a decade ago has also arrived. Of the three library sectors, academic libraries are the most active in hiring, with 46 percent of academic libraries hiring new librarians in 2003 (8Rs Research Team, p. 38).

Anecdotal evidence indicates that Canadian libraries are still hiring in both contract positions and continuing positions. Hiring on a contract basis is becoming routine for some libraries, particularly those located in a large city with a supply of librarians or those experiencing budgetary difficulties. 2003 data from the University of Alberta shows that fewer than 50 percent of their employed 2002 library school graduates held full-time continuing employment (Shrader). However, 70 to 75 percent of 2000 and 2001 graduates had full-time continuing employment. Many librarians in Canada who graduated after 1990 spent the initial part of their careers in temporary/contract positions and then found full-time continuing work. Fortunately, the impending retirement bubble should result in full-time continuing positions becoming available at academic libraries; this trend has already started. In the 1990s, some Canadian academic librarians (including the author of this chapter) opted to take advantage of NAFTA's Chapter 16 and headed to the U.S. after graduation to begin their careers. This practice has lessened as more new graduates find good academic jobs in Canada and as overall demand for librarians has increased (8Rs Research Team, p. 97).

Most advertisements for positions at Canadian academic libraries will include a statement such as "in accordance with Canadian Immigration requirements, this advertisement is initially directed to Canadian citizens and permanent residents of Canada" but U.S. librarians may still apply for Canadian jobs since Chapter 16 of NAFTA allows U.S., Canadian, or Mexican librarians to work in any of the NAFTA countries on a temporary work permit (Foreign Worker Manual, p. 75). This is not widely known in Canada; U.S. applicants should include this information in their cover letters. The process for entry to Canada is not as smooth as the process for going to the U.S. In 2002, an American colleague was denied a NAFTA permit for a two-week temporary job in Canada because a Canadian official felt that the employer could have found a qualified Canadian. The official, and perhaps the employer, was likely confused, as the requirement to look for a qualified Canadian employee does not apply under the NAFTA temporary work permit. Most academic librarian positions in Canada do not require a second master's degree, nor is there an expectation to obtain one.

The interview process for Canadian libraries is less intense than at many U.S. academic libraries. Where interviews at U.S. institutions may take one or two days and follow a faculty-like interview process, the Canadian norm is half a day and reflects the kinder, gentler view that Canadian librarians have of their academic status.

The library work of academic librarians in Canada and the U.S. is not radically different. Job responsibilities and organization of the library are very similar in the two countries. Both nations use the same library standards, including MARC, Anglo-American Cataloguing Rules, LC or Dewey classification, and the various NISO and ANSI standards.

Most librarians at Canadian universities and colleges have faculty or academic status, with a notable exception being the University of Waterloo (Ellis). Recent surveys of librarians in Canadian universities show that over 88 percent have either academic or faculty status (Millard, p. 103) compared to approximately 75 percent in the U.S. (Cary, p. 511). However, the faculty model prevalent in Canadian academic libraries emphasizes evaluative criteria based on job responsibilities rather than the traditional model based on research, teaching, and university service (Leckie and Brett, p. 39). Or, as an American colleague likes to call it, "faculty with a small 'f.' " This Canadian model stands in sharp contrast to U.S. academic libraries where the more traditional model is the norm for academic librarians with faculty status. This traditional faculty model is what most stood out to a Canadian biomedical librarian during her time at the University of Hawaii: "Everyone is expected to do research and the librarians are sometimes engaged in very independent projects and may not be as much a part of the public side of the library. I got the sense that the term 'faculty' is quite accurately applied to the librarians there. We are members of the faculty association here [Canada], but I don't think anyone would argue that we, as librarians, spend our time the same as most other faculty members." Few, if any, Canadian institutions use traditional faculty ranks for librarians. Instead, many Canadian university libraries use a ranking level of Librarian I, II, III, and IV (and even V) with promotion to the next level based on number of years of experience, type of job responsibilities, evaluation of professional job responsibilities, and contributions to the library profession. Librarian IV (and/or V) is usually reserved for librarians in administrative positions. Having experienced both a traditional promotion and tenure system in the U.S. and a Canadian evaluative system based on job responsibilities, I can state that the Canadian system is certainly less stressful, and promotion between levels easier to attain. This difference in faculty models results in less disparity between salaries and benefits among academic librarians in Canada, in contrast to the U.S., where the differences in faculty rank can significantly impact salaries and benefits (Leckie and Brett, p. 39).

Obtaining tenure, or a continuing position, at Canadian academic libraries is straightforward and based primarily on fulfilling professional job responsibilities and providing service to the library community through participation in library associations. Promotion is centered strongly on fulfilling professional job responsibilities, but definitely also includes research, publications, and service. Canadian academic librarians are encouraged to serve on university committees and to be active with library associations. This involvement and activity is important in obtaining promotion.

The less demanding Canadian faculty system for librarians has at least one drawback for the library community as a whole. Because they are not under the same pressure to publish as are U.S. librarians, there is little professional literature by Canadian librarians. Although Canadian academic librarians are active conference presenters, their publishing output is minimal, resulting in many

Canadian developments falling under the radar outside the Canadian library community.

Almost every Canadian university and college has unionized para-professional staff. In some universities, the faculty is also unionized. Colleges are somewhat different, as in most provinces the college faculty belong to a province-wide union. A strong union presence on Canadian post-secondary campuses creates a different dynamic than that found on many U.S. campuses, particularly for those in supervisory roles. Collective bargaining agreements strictly govern how staff hiring and promotions are carried out, how the workday is structured, and all other aspects of the job. Employee grievances are more likely to surface in a union environment. Work stoppages due to job action happen more frequently on Canadian campuses because action taken by one union will result in picket lines that unionized staff will not cross. On most campuses, there are two or three separate union locals representing the various staff, and these locals will belong to a large public-sector union. In the event of a staff strike, librarians are expected to carry out work such as circulation and shelving.

When I was at library school in British Columbia, one of my professors talked of the Vancouver and Victoria disease. By this, she meant that librarians were so eager to live in those two Canadian cities that they would get jobs there and never leave until retirement. Consequently, their careers stalled because no one else in the library was likely leaving before retirement either. This tendency is not limited to academic libraries in Vancouver and Victoria. In 1997, Leckie and Brett found that 62 percent of academic librarians in Canada have over fifteen years of experience (Leckie and Brett, p. 31) and Millard's 2001 survey found that of Canadian academic librarians surveyed with more than 15 years of experience, 58.8 percent had been at the same institution for over 20 years, and 80 percent had been at the same institution for more than 15 years (Millard, p. 105). These numbers are similar to Wilder's 1994 study, which found that 54 percent of all ARL librarians with 20 or more years of professional experience had worked at only one institution (Wilder). This does not invalidate the Canadian belief that U.S. librarians are more mobile than their Canadian counterparts, because the U.S. survey covers only large ARL libraries. Lower job mobility among Canadian librarians has the downside of reducing the number of new jobs on the market each year and reducing new blood coming into institutions.

However, it ensures the continuation of corporate memory and experience at Canadian academic institutions.

Canadian academic librarians are a happy bunch who enjoy their work; their job satisfaction is most influenced by the career itself and less by the personal and economic factors gained by working at an academic library (Millard, p. 106). Canadian and U.S. academic librarians both derive the most satisfaction from interactions with users and peers and from their assigned responsibilities—that is, from the traditional roles of librarianship (Horenstein, p. 264; Leckie and Brett, p. 44). A departure between Canadian and U.S. academic librarians is in the fulfillment felt by having academic status. Faculty status, though important to academic librarians in Canada, does not relate as strongly to job satisfaction as it does in the United States (Leckie, p. 38). Faculty status does not seem to affect librarian satisfaction with salary and benefits, or their relationship with administration and involvement with library management (Leckie and Brett, p. 39). Academic status librarians in Canada do not perceive themselves to be more in control of their work, more involved with decision making, nor more in-the-loop on library matters (Leckie and Brett, p. 41). South of the border, Horenstein's 1993 study found significant differences in satisfaction between faculty and nonfaculty librarians, including that faculty librarians felt more involved and had better salaries (Horenstein, p. 265). In fact, Horenstein states that "key predictors of job satisfaction of academic librarians are perception of participation, salary, and possession of academic rank"—all of which are dependent on having faculty status (Horenstein, p. 264).

Canadian Copyright

The Canadian Copyright Act differs from U.S. copyright in ways that affect libraries negatively. The Canadian Copyright Act lacks the Fair Use provisions and educational exemptions of U.S. copyright law, and there are no educational fair use guidelines agreed to by publishers and the academic community, like Circular 21 from the U.S. Copyright Office. Canadian government publications are not in the public domain, but rather the copyright is held by the government and called Crown Copyright. On the positive side, copyright in Canada only lasts for 50 years after the death of the creator, a shorter term than is found in U.S. copyright. The Canadian version of Fair Use is called Fair Dealing and involves copying of insubstantial amounts of a work, for purposes of research, private study, criticism, review, or news reporting. Insubstantial copying is usually considered to allow copying of between 1 to 2 percent of a work, but not if that 1 to 2 percent is the key to the whole work or a famous part of the work. Unfortunately, the limits of Fair Dealing are not spelled out in the Canadian Copyright Act. Instead, it is something that the courts determine when the copyright owner sues. Articles from scholarly journals and those from newspapers and other periodicals that are over a year old may be copied for research or private study.

The tight photocopying restrictions of Fair Dealing resulted in the formation of CANCOPY—now called Access Copyright—a collective of creators and publishers that administers the legal rights of, and collects and distributes money to, the rights holders of print works. As such, it licenses educational institutions, businesses, and government to allow legal copying well beyond the confines of Fair Dealing. The Association of Universities and Colleges of Canada negotiates the Access Copyright licence for post-secondary institutions in Canada, including the price per FTE student that determines how much each institution will pay. Some examples of what the Access Copyright license allows is the copying of: up to 10 percent of a published work; one chapter from a book; entire short stories, essays, and poems; entire newspaper or periodical articles regardless of age; and an entire artistic work reproduced in a book or periodical (Kornfeld, p. 5). Because every college and university pays for an Access Copyright license, faculty and students get confused about the limits of Fair Dealing and think that the Access Copyright rules are in fact Fair Dealing. Access Copyright covers only print materials.

No educational exemptions for film and video exist in the Canadian Copyright Act. Consequently, a legal copy of a video cannot be shown in a face-to-face teaching situation unless it comes with nontheatrical public performance rights. Naturally, public performance rights come with a price. In the area of feature films, licensing again provides a solution as two companies, between them, license most Hollywood and some foreign feature films for Canadian institutions. The licenses are annual and the price is based on FTE students. Other films, if used in the classroom, must be purchased with public performance rights. Unfortunately, public performance rights can be difficult, or impossible, to obtain for many foreign films. The work required to obtain the rights for one video can take media librarians hours or days of work. Alas, faculty members are often unaware of Canadian copyright restrictions on cinematographic works, and therefore show the films in the class with or without public performance rights. There is also flagrant disregard for public performance rights, which is understandable when you consider how difficult the Canadian Copyright Act makes it to use film and video in face-to-face teaching.

Canadian copyright requires that interlibrary loans be delivered to the end user in paper format. Although the document can be transmitted between libraries in electronic format, the receiving library must print out the document for pick up by the patron and destroy the electronic file. U.S. copyright law, contrary to what many Americans think, takes a more balanced approach to the rights of creators and consumers than does the Canadian Copyright Act, which is weighted almost entirely in favor of the creator. Wanda Noel, a well known Canadian copyright lawyer, puts it best when she says "library staff should remember that fair dealing should not be confused with the much broader American concept of fair use" (Noel, 28).

Collection Development and Collection Management Issues

Approximately 80 percent of works in Canadian academic library collections are foreign (Flagg). Since the vast majority of foreign works are priced in U.S. dollars regardless of place of publication, Canadian academic libraries collection budgets are primarily expended in U.S. dollars. This means that Canadian academic libraries face two funding challenges—the usual institutional funding issues and currency exchange rate fluctuations. If the Canadian dollar drops against the U.S. dollar, the collections budget purchasing power falls; if the dollar rises then the purchasing power goes up. In the late 1990s, the Canadian dollar plummeted versus the U.S. dollar, wreaking havoc with collections budgets. Suddenly everyone experienced a defacto budget cut. Although in some cases the library budget actually increased, no increase was enough to offset the fall in the Canadian dollar. In 2003, the Canadian dollar started to rise, and suddenly, with no budget increase, Canadian academic libraries had more money to spend. I constantly did currency conversions when looking at prices. When I worked in the U.S., I had to keep reminding myself that the budget I was working with was in U.S. dollars, and so was everything I was buying! Until you have experienced it, it is hard to imagine the simple joy of being able to buy in the currency your budget is set in.

Most major publishers in the North American market require Canadians to deal with their U.S. offices. Licenses for electronic resources must be modified to reflect Canadian rather than U.S. laws, and to reflect the Canadian academic scene. One major example is license language regarding multiple campuses. In Canada, a university with multiple campuses means the university has a single main campus with one or two dependent satellite campuses. It does not mean a University of California system or a State University of New York system. Many licenses are renegotiated around this wording, usually resulting in raised cultural awareness on both sides.

The dependence of Canadian academic libraries on foreign works results in extra effort on the part of academic librarians to ensure that Canadian works are collected, publicized, and used. In a way, they become guardians of Canadian culture.

Canada's small population and vast geography make consortia a necessity. Two main differences between the U.S. and Canada are the smaller ratio of consortia per library in Canada and the presence of a national consortium in Canada. The Canadian Research Knowledge Network, originally known as the Canadian National Site Licensing Project, is a national consortium that licenses a variety of Big Deals at the national level and is comprised of the 64 Canadian universities. In its first three years, the consortium had 50 million dollars in a federal grant, but now the consortium depends on member libraries for all funding. The benefit of a national consortium is the negotiating power that comes with representing an entire country. One result is that the archival provisions for the electronic journals are very good and allow the member libraries to cancel print without concerns about continuing access. The Canadian Research Knowledge Network has allowed Canadian university libraries access to many more e-journals and has resulted in high levels of satisfaction among researchers and librarians at Canadian universities (Impact Group, p. 41).

Professional Organizations

The Canadian Library Association is not as dominant in Canada as the ALA is in the U.S. This is due partly to the size of the Ontario Library Association. Ontario has 33 percent of Canada's population and the OLA, with almost as many members as the entire CLA, has an annual conference that rivals CLA's annual conference. The Canadian library world is small and many librarians belong to one of the larger U.S.-based international library organizations such as the Special Libraries Association or Medical Libraries Association. To a lesser extent, they also belong to ALA. The international library organizations are important for Canadian librarians because they extend the network of professional contacts, have multiple Canadian chapters, and provide support unavailable from smaller Canadian library organizations.

Works Cited

8Rs Research Team. *Future of Heritage Work in Canada (DRAFT)*. Edmonton: University of Alberta, 2004. Available 19 May 2004: www.cdncouncilarchives. ca/events/ 8RsFutureofHeritageWorkDRAFT.pdf

Canadian Subject Headings. 7 Jan. 2004. Library and Archives Canada. Available 18 May 2004: www.lac-bac.gc.ca/csh/index-e.html

Cary, Shannon. "Faculty Rank, Status, and Tenure for Librarians." *College and Research Library News*, 62.5 (2001): 510–511.

Durand, M. "Average Annual Growth Rate of 5% for Culture Occupations in the Culture Sector, 1991 to 2002." *Focus on Culture*, 14.3 (2004): 1–8.

Ellis, P. "UWO Professional Librarians and Archivists Join UWOFA." *Faculty Times: A Newsletter of the University of Western Ontario Faculty Association*, 8.3 (2004). Available 29 June 2004: www.uwo.ca/uwofa/ft/8.3/ ellis

Flagg, Gordon et al. "Libraries North and South of the Border." *American Libraries Online: ALA Midwinter Meeting 2003 Report*, 2003. Available 25 April 2004: archive.ala.org/alonline/news/midwinter03.html#border

Foreign Worker Manual. Appendix G—North American Free Trade Agreement (NAFTA). 10 Sept. 2003. Citizenship and Immigration Canada. Available 25 May 2004: www.cic.gc.ca/manuals-guides/english/fw/fwe.pdf

Horenstein, Bonnie. "Job Satisfaction of Academic Librarians: An Examination of the Relationships between Satisfaction and Participation." *College and Research Libraries*, 54.3 (1993): 255–269.

Impact Group. *Impact of the Canadian National Site Licensing Project: A Report to Stakeholders*. 2004.

Kornfeld, Judy, and Niina Mitter. *Copyright Guide*. Vancouver: Langara College, 2001.

Leckie, Gloria J., and Jim Brett. "Job Satisfaction of Canadian University Librarians: A National Survey." *College and Research Libraries*, 58.1 (1997): 31–47.

Millard, Donna. "Why Do We Stay? Survey of Long-Term Academic Librarians in Canada." *Portal: Libraries and the Academy*, 3.1 (2003): 99–111.

Noel, Wanda. *Copyright Guide for Canadian Libraries*. Ottawa: Canadian Library Association, 1999.

Schrader, Alvin. *U of A SLIS Employment Survey, 2002 Graduates*, Dec. 2003. School of Library and Information Studies, University of Alberta. Available 20 June 2004: www.slis.ualberta.ca/report02.htm

Wilder, Stanley. "The Age Demographics of Academic Librarians." *ARL: A Bimonthly Newsletter of Research Library Issues and Actions*, 185 (1996). Available 29 May 2004: www.arl.org/newsltr/185/agedemo.html

Part 3

Tales from the Trenches— Academic Librarians Share Their Stories

CHAPTER 12

Notes From a Cataloger—
Success in Technical Services

Wendy Baia

> *"A university is a historic wager that people of different beliefs can sustain passionate conversations."*
> —Michael Brooks

Imagine you wake up each weekday morning looking forward to the new challenges that await you at work. You have confidence that you will be able to handle any difficult problems that you confront. You work in a library with a collegial atmosphere where you like and respect your supervisor and colleagues and where you are respected and liked. You use your intelligence and skills in a position that has just the right amount of challenge. You make useful contributions that are appreciated and improve the library service at your institution. You believe your salary and benefits are fair compensation for your efforts. Your work provides deep personal satisfaction, and your life is in balance.

Most librarians would probably agree that this scenario contains many of the important ingredients for job satisfaction. However, few of us attain such a situation without experiencing many difficulties along the way. Each life journey is unique; there is not any one formula for success. We can learn skills and techniques to maximize our probability of success. All of the information in this chapter can help academic librarians in any type of position. The emphasis is on a nontenure track position, and most of my examples come from technical services, because this is where my experience lies. I have held nontenure track positions in three university libraries for a total of thirty years.

I began my career as a serials cataloger at Syracuse University. My goal was to hold a position in reference or collection development in a university library. I was relocating to Syracuse, New York, and Syracuse University was the obvious choice for library employment. The one position open at that time was a beginning serials cataloger position. I was offered this job and happily accepted it. Although cataloging—what I knew of it from my one cataloging class in library school—was not my first choice, there were certain aspects of cataloging that attracted me, especially classification and the assignment of subject headings. What did not attract me about cataloging was the arbitrariness and fussiness of some descriptive cataloging rules. As I became an experienced serials cataloger, I discovered a whole new fascinating world where I could use my analytical and problem solving skills to solve an endless stream of serials cataloging problems. Providing user-friendly cataloging became a source of deep satisfaction. A specialty that I did not know existed when I chose my career as a librarian became my life's work and thirty-seven years later it continues to provide challenges that I enjoy conquering.

I continued my career in serials cataloging following family relocations—first to Ann Arbor at the University of Michigan from 1974–1986 and then to Boulder at the University of Colorado from 1989 to the present. I was promoted to Head of Serials Cataloging in 1990 and Assistant Head of the Cataloging Department in 2001, and appointed the Interim Head of Cataloging in 2002. I have now been a supervisor and middle manager for fourteen years. I have supervised and trained dozens of faculty and staff in serials cataloging, have served on numerous search committees, several of which I chaired, attended more meetings than I care to remember, and have been active on numerous library committees. From the first day of my first library job, I have been interested in understanding as much as possible about library operations outside my own department and fulfilling my responsibilities in the larger context of my library's goals and mission. This experience has provided me with valuable knowledge of the organizational culture of academic libraries.

Defining Success in Academic Librarianship

Money, fame, and power are the big three symbols of success in the business, entertainment, and sports worlds. These are generally not the top motivations for a career choice in academic librarianship. In an academic library, how far one has risen in the hierarchy is considered by some as indicative of your success. Most would probably agree that those who achieve the position of library director or assistant director and those who are heads of departments must have attained a certain level of success to hold these positions. Because not everyone has a managerial or top administrative position as a goal, other measures of success are more meaningful to some individuals. Being recognized for one's expertise and believing one's contributions have made a positive difference contribute to a sense of personal success no matter where you are in the hierarchy or what your title is.

Circumstances of family life, children, and outside interests often greatly alter the goals you had at the start of a career as well as your definition of success. Many factors can influence whether you pursue positions in which career advancement, which some might interpret as greater success, is more likely. These include a spouse or partner who does not want to relocate, the desire to stay in an area close to family and friends, and an unwillingness to uproot children. If a librarian stays in the same position for a long time, no matter how experienced and competent, it is essential that he or she keeps growing in the job, adapting to change, and acquiring new skills to avoid stagnation. Job success is not something you achieve one exhilarating day, after which you can rest on your laurels.

Your ability to succeed depends on choosing a work environment where your values and goals match those of the library administration and your colleagues. You may be superb at your job in your own eyes, but if your accomplishments are not valued in your library, you will not succeed at that institution. The vision and priorities of the library director and upper level managers as well as your direct supervisor are supremely important. If you are an innovative and creative person, you will be happiest where innovation and creativity are valued and rewarded. Conversely, a librarian with a traditional orientation may be most content where there is not constant experimentation and standards are not commonly ignored.

Being a team player also contributes to success in most academic libraries. In *The 7 Habits of Highly Effective People*, Stephen R. Covey discusses what he calls "interdependence" as a far more mature method of interaction with others to achieve success than either dependence or independence. Covey describes interdependent people as self-reliant and capable, yet able to cooperate with others to achieve more than could be achieved alone. In your library position, speaking your truth is vital to maintain your integrity, but it is important to pick your battles and use diplomacy and consideration for others in expressing your views. The importance of taking the high road when striving for success cannot be underestimated. You will encounter numerous examples of perceived unfairness: your raise was not as large as someone else's was, someone misinterpreted a comment you made, an accomplishment is not acknowledged. How you deal with these situations indicates your maturity. Showing kindness to others, sharing your knowledge, not taking yourself too seriously and treating all your coworkers with respect are traits of a mature, confident individual.

As you have read in previous chapters, academic status/rank and expectations for librarians can vary considerably among institutions. Just because a position is nontenure track does not automatically mean that research and service are of little importance. If they are a significant component, your success in these areas may depend on how much support is provided for these activities—in the amount of time allotted to do research on the job, time and financial support to attend conferences, and mentoring for those new at research.

Anyone in a nontenure track position in a library with tenure track positions will most definitely be affected by the demands placed on their tenure track colleagues. Extensive time spent on research is time that is not available for the daily library tasks. Nontenure track librarians may become resentful of extra burdens placed on them because their tenure track colleagues may have to spend a large proportion of their time fulfilling their research and service obligations. Being respectful and understanding of the demands faced by all colleagues as they diligently attempt to fulfill their responsibilities is essential for harmony and productivity as we work together as colleagues.

Possessing expertise in an academic library specialty is essential for success in that specialty, but it is rarely sufficient, particularly if one wishes to attain a supervisory or upper level position. A combination of interpersonal skills, communication skills, organizational skills, and supervisory skills is also essential. It has been my observation that even though these skills are usually listed as job requirements, often much less attention and effort is focused on them, to the detriment of overall job performance. The erroneous belief that these skills just come naturally rather than requiring any special attention or training can limit success. Some of these skills are easier for some than others, but no one is automatically an expert in one or more of these areas without considerable effort and experience.

During my library career, I have been fortunate to work at universities that offered numerous free workshops in many skills areas. Some of the workshops I've attended are: writing skills improvement, interviewing, public speaking, coping with change, communication, conflict management, teamwork, time management, effective meetings, Total Quality Management, art of negotiation, assertive supervision, internal customer service, diversity, sexual harassment for supervisors, ergonomics, Feng Shui for work, and stress management. Several of these I have taken more than once. I consider attendance at these workshops worthwhile as long as I gain one significant piece of advice to enhance my job performance. It was rare for absolutely nothing I learned to be of any use on the job or in other areas of my life.

Once an individual recognizes the importance of these skills and is motivated to improve expertise in them, she will find no shortage of guidance available. I highly recommend Judith A. Siess's *Time Management, Planning, and Prioritization for Librarians*. Besides the topics in the title, it also covers ways to improve communication, interpersonal relations, and stress reduction. Although geared for the special librarian, the information has strong applicability for academic librarians. If every beginning academic librarian received a copy of this book, or one like it, with their packet of essential information on arrival at their first job, their road to success would be significantly easier. Another book full of helpful suggestions for new librarians is Priscilla K. Shontz's *Jump Start Your Career in Library and Information Science*.

Challenges of Communication in a Hierarchical Institution

The larger the institution and the more complex the hierarchy, the more communication problems develop. Common complaints in academic libraries are "The right hand doesn't know what the left hand is doing" and "Nobody consulted with me before this decision was made." In every university library where I have worked, many staff members consider communication a problem. Communication problems are generally acknowledged, but finding solutions is a continual process of trial and error.

Knowing who needs to be involved or informed and at what point they need to be involved or informed in decisions on new policies, practices, and procedures requires judgment that is often learned the hard way. When you neglect to consult someone or forget to inform others of decisions that affect them, the negative reaction is usually swift. The solution is to analyze carefully who needs to be consulted beforehand and who needs to be informed of the decision. You also need to decide the best medium of communication: meeting one-on-one or with a few of those most closely involved, meeting with a whole unit or department, forming a committee or task force, sending a written message, or using e-mail. Two of the most popular yet potentially troublesome forms of communication are e-mail and meetings.

E-mail is an efficient way to communicate with a group, gathering input and informing others of decisions and policies. People can read your e-mail at a time that is convenient for them. When used wisely, e-mail is a wonderful time-saver, but it can easily be abused. Some people send messages on e-mail that they would never send otherwise. Professional lists help keep us current with the latest developments in our field, but there is a danger in becoming absorbed in threads that contain minutia of little real significance. If you are someone who writes e-mails that are well thought out and as brief as possible to convey appropriate significant messages and only forwards e-mails judiciously, your colleagues and supervisors will be appreciative.

Holding a meeting is a better mechanism for discussions of complex issues when e-mails become excessively lengthy and confusing. Unfortunately, running an effective meeting is a skill not everyone has. Some meetings deteriorate into complaint sessions or lengthy exchanges of non-work related banter. Several years ago, our library established a task force to look into the problem of excessive meetings. The number of meetings held on a regular basis was tallied and guidance was provided for holding efficient meetings. Preparing an agenda prior to a meeting, staying on topic, making sure no one person dominates the meeting and that everyone who wants to participate has a chance to contribute, and keeping meetings as short as possible to accomplish goals of the meeting help assure productive, efficient meetings. Surprisingly, an attempt to reduce the frequency of some regular meetings, such as a department meeting, can meet with resistance. People complain that too many meetings cut into their productive work time, but if you try to eliminate them or cut back, you may receive complaints that a valued means of two-way communication will be lost.

One of the best books on communication I have read is *How the Way We Talk Can Change the Way We Work: Seven Languages for Transformation* by Robert Kegan and Lisa Laskow Lahey. They discuss impediments to successful communication for individuals and organizations and present a clear plan to overcome resistance to change. For example, their first recommendation teaches us how to change from the language of complaint to the language of commitment. They describe this as going from the negativity of what we cannot stand to positive energizing expressions of what we stand for. I learned about this book in a newsletter on the Web site of an expert in Integral Coaching and Leadership Training, who also happens to be my oldest son. Never underestimate the power of serendipity and synchronicity on your road to success!

Cooperation to Save the Time of the User

Cooperation between public services and technical services is essential to achieve library goals. Problems develop when public services employees do not clearly articulate their needs to technical services employees or technical services employees do not consider the ultimate purpose of the tasks they undertake as they relate to library goals. I used to joke to myself that I stayed in cataloging this long because I'd be too frustrated to be a public services librarian who had to deal with some rigid catalogers who consider the "perfect" catalog record as an end in itself rather than the means to connect users with the resources they're seeking. As our online catalogs have become more complex and sophisticated, cooperation between technical services and public services employees becomes even more critical. Catalogers who respond to public services needs by providing accurate, clear, and helpful catalog records are held in high regard by their public services colleagues.

Catalogers can also show initiative by organizing workshops designed for public services staff. When I became Head of Serials

Cataloging in 1990, I began holding workshops to help library employees in both public and technical services search serial records efficiently and interpret catalog records. Over the years I have organized and conducted workshops in a variety of formats, including large one-session workshops and small group sessions. One of my more adventuresome undertakings was a series of customized workshops where, along with a staff member, I went to individual branches and units and used examples from their collections, so that the workshop would be as relevant as possible to the needs of that unit. An example of a recent workshop conducted by representatives of our library's Cataloging Department was "Demystifying Chinook Bibliographic Records." (Chinook is the name of our OPAC.) This was a well-attended session, and we received many expressions of appreciation.

Most academic libraries have committees and task forces with technical services and public services representation. These provide a wonderful opportunity to work together and see different perspectives. You will get to know colleagues that you might not otherwise know on more than a superficial level. If you believe cooperation between public services and technical services needs improvement, work to be part of the solution rather than part of the problem.

Supervision

Early in my career I suggested a procedure change that I thought would improve cataloging efficiency. The response I received from the head of the department was, "We have spent years building this system up. Why are you trying to break it down?" What was the suggestion that would wreak havoc on the whole operation? I suggested eliminating certain nonessential information on a series authority file card. At this same library I was later severely castigated by my supervisor for adding a hand-written note to a printed instruction sheet that catalogers gave to the Catalog Management Unit to indicate changes to be made to cards in the catalog. I was told I was not at liberty to modify established procedures and had to conform by checking the appropriate box only, with no additions to the printed instruction sheet.

These incidents stick in my mind because they shocked and mortified me at the time and then helped shape the kind of supervisor I became. I learned from these two incidents that supervisors often have a personal investment in the procedures and practices they created and will not always welcome suggestions for change, no matter how beneficial. Thus, it can be extremely important how you offer suggestions, so they are not perceived as criticism of the current system. The best supervisors actively solicit suggestions for improvement, but are aware that even those who say they welcome suggestions may not actually accept change when it affects something they have created.

A good supervisor is aware of the varying skills of those she supervises. She attempts to match these abilities with the responsibilities of her unit. She is approachable and behaves in a friendly professional manner. A sense of humor can help lighten any difficult situation and relieve everyday stresses. A good supervisor praises in public and criticizes only in private. If a supervisor acts overwhelmed by her tasks, this increases the stress in the unit. After assuring that those she supervises have received training and documentation for the tasks they must perform, a good supervisor is available to answer questions and for consultation on problems that need her attention, but she doesn't micromanage competent trustworthy employees.

A good employee follows the established chain of command, whenever possible. She is flexible and volunteers to take on additional duties when needed. She is loyal to her unit and keeps her supervisor informed of current activities and the status of projects. When she comes to her supervisor to discuss problems, she has suggestions for solutions. If she is doing something that she does not understand, she asks questions to avoid making mistakes out of ignorance. If one of her duties does not make sense, she asks why it is being done rather than mindlessly continuing to do it. She treats her supervisors and coworkers with respect. Misunderstandings occur when we make erroneous assumptions, so she verifies information when in doubt.

Library Leadership and Change

Leaders are individuals with vision who are not afraid to take risks to achieve their goals. Brooke E. Sheldon, author of *Leaders in Libraries: Styles and Strategies for Success*, interviewed sixty leaders in the library profession, including many directors of academic libraries, to identify qualities and strategies that led to their success.

These library leaders were results-oriented, able to articulate their goals, and able to motivate others to accomplish them. Sheldon describes the leader's job as deciding what should be done and leaving to others how it will be done.

Because academic library directors generally prefer to concentrate on the big picture and not get bogged down in details, other librarians in the organization can make a strong impact by also having vision accompanied by the ability to implement needed changes. Those who move ahead in their careers are the people who view change as a challenge rather than an obstacle. They welcome the opportunity to acquire new knowledge and skills and assist others in learning. We all have acquaintances and coworkers who bemoan the rapidly accelerating rate of change. They complain about all the things that need to be learned and the training they never received to learn them. Coping with the constant need to adapt to new technology can be a continual source of frustration.

A positive aspect of constant change is that it creates opportunities for new leaders and experts in new areas. Most supervisors will be grateful to employees who step forward and show initiative. New practices need to be developed and new procedures written. The library needs someone to be in charge of a special project or a task force to implement a new system. If you are an energetic person who enthusiastically pursues new challenges and takes a leadership role in implementing them, you will be viewed as an asset in your library. You can also emerge as a functional expert in some new area. Be a positive force in how the future unfolds in your library, rather than a passive onlooker, disgruntled when things do not turn out as you expected.

Stress and the Library

Do your best! Give 100%! Be all you can be! These maxims can inspire the determination, commitment, and fortitude that contribute to success. However well intentioned, they can also have undesirable consequences when taken to extremes. In *Stress and Burnout in Library Service*, librarian and clinical psychologist Janette S. Caputo lists five personal characteristics that make a person vulnerable to burnout: high idealism, perfectionism, overcommitment, single-mindedness, and lack of personal support. How much do you have to do to do your best? How hard do you have to try to give 100 percent? A helpful guideline comes from the principle of "right effort," the sixth factor of the Noble Eightfold Path in Buddhism. This is explained by Joseph Goldstein in Tony Schwartz's *What Really Matters: Searching for Wisdom in America* as the quality of being "persistent and persevering but with a relaxed and balanced mind, making the effort without forcing" (p. 321).

In addition to individual qualities that lead to burnout, there are sources of stress in our libraries, including declining budgets, constant change, poor communication, lack of needed training, interpersonal problems, ill-equipped supervisors, inefficient managers, and too much work with too few workers. Having responsibility without the authority to make decisions and implement them is a well-known contributor to stress. Because stress is inevitable, it is essential to be aware when it affects your job performance, job satisfaction, and the quality of your life. You need to take steps to bring your life in balance. Strategies for stress reduction are almost as varied as the sources of stress. You can find suggestions for stress reduction in the daily newspaper, popular magazines, TV news shows, popular books, tapes, CDs, workshops, and professional literature. If you're still not quite sure where to start, a book that provides practical easy-to-adopt suggestions is *Inner Peace for Busy People: 52 Simple Strategies for Transforming Your Life* by Joan Borysenko, a leader in mind-body medicine. Another source of inspiration to restore inner tranquility is *Practicing the Power of Now: Essential Teachings, Meditations, and Exercises from The Power of Now* by Eckhart Tolle. Tolle tells us, "You can always cope with the Now, but you can never cope with the future—nor do you have to. The answer, the strength, the right action, or the resource will be there when you need it, not before, not after" (p. 51). In *Positive Energy: 10 Extraordinary Prescriptions for Transforming Fatigue, Stress, and Fear into Vibrance, Strength, and Love,* psychiatrist Judith Orloff includes a chapter on opening the flow of inspiration and creativity with suggestions to re-inspire our jobs.

One further cause of stress deserves special mention. A full-time academic librarian who is also raising young children is almost certain to experience the stress of juggling these two demanding responsibilities. I was fortunate to be able to work part-time as an academic librarian while each of my three children was young. This was the perfect solution, enabling me to devote not only quality time but also enough time to my children while still maintaining my commitment as a librarian. Not everyone can afford this, but if you can, consider it. I have found academic libraries to be flexible and accommodating once you have proved your worth to your library.

Conclusion

The road to success in a library begins before you are hired. Choose a library position consistent with your philosophy of service. Interviews for positions are not just for the library to decide on the best-qualified candidate, but also for the candidate to decide if the library is a good fit with her goals and values. Are new ideas and innovations welcome? Do the employees appear enthusiastic and energetic or bored and discouraged? How complex is the chain of command? How are decisions made? Which meetings must you attend and which are optional? What is the evaluation process? How are your salary increases determined? If you are a nontenure track librarian in a library that also has tenure track faculty, will you feel like a second-class citizen or will you be treated with equal respect? Is there support for research and service if you wish to engage in these activities?

Once you have obtained your first academic librarian position, your motivation, job knowledge and skills, personality, character traits, and sometimes just being in the right place at the right time affect the success you achieve. Do not underestimate the importance of good interpersonal, communication, organizational, time management, and supervisory skills. Develop your leadership skills by seeing the big picture and becoming involved with cooperative library activities. Whenever there is a choice, take the high road. Share your knowledge, do not take yourself too seriously, treat all your coworkers with kindness and respect, learn from your mistakes, and laugh at the inevitable absurdities. Adopt strategies to cope with stress and keep your life in balance. Remember the words of Alan Kay, the originator of the laptop computer: "The best way to predict the future is to invent it."

Works Cited

Borysenko, Joan. *Inner Peace for Busy People: 52 Simple Strategies for Transforming Your Life*. Carlsbad, CA: Hay House, 2001.

Caputo, Janette S. *Stress and Burnout in Library Service.* Phoenix, AZ: Oryx Press, 1991.

Covey, Stephen R. *The 7 Habits of Highly Effective People: Restoring the Character Ethic.* New York: Simon and Schuster, 1989.

Kegan, Robert, and Lisa Laskow Lahey. *How the Way We Talk Can Change the Way We Work: Seven Languages for Transformation.* San Francisco: Jossey-Bass, 2001.

Library Literature & Information Science Full Text. Bronx, NY: H. W. Wilson. WilsonWeb. 12 Jul 2004.

Orloff, Judith. *Positive Energy: 10 Extraordinary Prescriptions for Transforming Fatigue, Stress, and Fear into Vibrance, Strength, and Love.* New York: Harmony Books, 2004.

Schwartz, Tony. *What Really Matters: Searching for Wisdom in America.* New York: Bantam Books, 1995.

Sheldon, Brooke E. *Leaders in Libraries: Styles and Strategies for Success.* Chicago: American Library Association, 1991.

Shontz, Priscilla K. *Jump Start Your Career in Library and Information Science.* Lanham, MD: Scarecrow Press, 2002.

Siess, Judith A. *Time Management, Planning and Prioritization for Librarians.* Lanham, MD: Scarecrow Press, 2002.

Tolle, Eckhart. *Practicing the Power of Now: Essential Teachings, Meditations, and Exercises from The Power of Now.* Novato, CA: New World Library, 1999.

CHAPTER 13

Witches Brew or Gourmet Gumbo—Tenure in the Library

Molly E. Molloy

"University politics are vicious precisely because the stakes are so small."
—Henry Kissinger (1923–)

Prologue

From: Molly
To: Miles
Dear Miles—I wonder if you remember me? I was a student of yours back in the early '70s. I think a lot of you and your work. I'm still proud of my poetry from Nicaragua that you published many years ago in *Anthropology and Humanism* ... although the library dean here a while back said it wouldn't help me get tenure and I should take it off my vita. ... I left it on and I got tenure anyway! And he is no longer dean. Thanks!

From: Miles
To: Molly
Subject: Of Course!
Molly,
I remember you so well. Good for you to keep the poems on your vita! What did that dean know! What a great outcome, you get tenure and he's gone. A poem right there! Thanks so much for keeping in touch.
With warm smiles from poet to poet, and person to person.
Miles[1]

It Should Always Taste Good, Even Though It Might Not Look Like the Picture in the Magazine

I always thought that someday I would write a cookbook. I love to cook and can hardly remember a time when I did not do it. I became self-conscious about my kitchen-life in junior high when my big brother would interrupt my enthusiastic whippings and stirrings with a singsong taunt, "Little Miss Home-Ec." Oh, it was awful. I'd always been a tomboy and a far better outdoorsman than my science-geek brother (too bad the geek word wasn't available to me then), but he managed to rip up my self-image, dressing me with his words in apron, flour-dustings, lipstick, and frump. It didn't matter. I still cooked, read recipe books, perused the ladies' magazines at the dentist's office, watched my mother (and father) in the kitchen, and argued with them and with my home economics teacher, who lived across the street from me and was one of the worst cooks I've ever known. That is a hard thing to be in south Louisiana.

What does this have to do with my contribution to *The Successful Academic Librarian*? Well, I have not yet written my cookbook, mainly because I can never seem to cook the same dish more than once exactly the same way. Given that recipes must be tested and replicable, I cannot figure out how to write a cookbook that would guarantee my readers similar results in the kitchen. So it goes that neither can I write a book of recipes for success as an academic librarian. I have done a few things in that realm that could be called successful. I earned tenure and have been promoted twice at a mid-sized public university. What have I learned from this process that I can pass on here? It will not be a recipe, because I do not know how to write them to guarantee consistent results. I can talk about what I have learned from my elders, mentors, bosses, and colleagues. I can tell you how I have argued with my elders, mentors, bosses, and colleagues. I believe that I can pass on something about ingredients that are not secret at all, but that are essential, sometimes tasty, and always hard to measure.

Priorities Are Made to Be Straight, Not Crooked

First, let us decide something about the relationship between survival and living. In order to get on with living, one must figure out survival, which for most of us (unless we get very lucky in lottery-land or romance-land) means ensuring some kind of job security. In terms of academic librarianship, this often means finding a path through the promotion and tenure process that will facilitate survival and at the same time allow us to enjoy the job and even live a life that is not too squeezed dry by the requisites of the process.

I must recount an anecdote from my first year at my library. We were a contingent of first and second year faculty librarians, locked inside the closed library all Labor Day weekend, anxiously writing, printing, photocopying, and organizing (with colored tabs) our contributions to librarianship, research, publication and creative activity, and service, and compiling multiple copies of everything to turn in by the Monday deadline. Our *ad nauseum* discussion of the P&T process deteriorated to the point that one colleague assigned the words "puke and tremble" to the acronym.

Unfortunately, for the first few years that I worked my way through the process, I never got that "puke and tremble" feeling to go away. It was especially bad during the days and weeks of the fall semester when I frantically worked to prepare my document and then awaited judgment from the formidable P&T Committee, a group at the time composed of all of the faculty members in the library who already had tenure. After a year or so, I learned that some members of the fearsome committee had never gone through the process in quite the way I understood it. Rather, they had earned their coveted "continuous contracts" simply by being there. They wrote guidelines and procedures and compiled them all into a big manual given to each new librarian. They met each year to sit in judgment on whether a lowly hireling like me could continue to live and work for another year in this place I had decided to call home. I was a single parent with six years behind me chasing jobs and graduate school from coast to coast with several stops in the swamps and deserts along the way. The idea of finding a home and a school and a community that my kid could grow up in was a very valuable thing. No way I would let a *committee* take it away! As far as I could tell, many of them had not done many of the demanding professional, creative and serviceable things that I assumed (by reading their manual of guidelines and procedures) were required to get that permanent job here—to be deemed a worthy academic professional librarian at our university. Just what might their real criteria for judgment be? Could my stomach stand it?

If any of my colleagues who made up these committees over the years should happen to read this, they will most likely be righteously indignant to think that their juniors thought (or think) of them in such terms. Or will they? I cannot say that this is a universal aspect of promotion and tenure in academic libraries, but our committee and our process persist in my memory (and in anecdotal evidence gathered from my colleagues past and present) as a social entity designed to foment stress and wreak emotional havoc upon those who must pass through it. I am speaking as not only a formerly disgruntled tenure seeker, but also as a successful tenured librarian with many years of active service on our P&T committee.

Who Let Those Creatures Out of the Box?
Or, How Did Those Ideas Get Into My Head?

I remember how, in my early years, members of the committee would assure us untenured folks that they were not to be feared: that they were really our mentors, that they wanted everyone to succeed. After my requisite six years of striving and the same number of annual P&T documents, growing thicker and grander and finally requiring a large file box for (always timely) delivery to the dean and the committee, I got my coveted continuous contract. The rewards are wonderful—job security, a nice raise, the idea that your colleagues consider you worth having around for a while (maybe forever), the idea that buying a house (instead of renting yet another student-ghetto apartment) is not the same as jumping out of a small plane without a parachute. With all of these benefits comes the responsibility of mentoring and judging my junior colleagues as a new member of the awesome committee.

I'm happy to report that the composition and character of promotion and tenure committees in our library continues to change, to grow, to evolve, but those first few years were difficult for me. I sat in meetings, discussing the merits and demerits of the people with whom I spent so many hours of my life. I closed my eyes at the meeting table and suddenly I could see little demons swirling around the room and landing on our heads with spidery sharp talons. They peered at us with hot yellow eyes, leaned their slimy green tongues close to our ears and spewed out raspy chatter that then magically emerged from our own mouths, sounding like our own voices, saying things like: Should these newsletter articles or book reviews be counted as publications? This person's article has been "accepted for publication" for four years but did it ever come out in the journal? That book chapter really does not count because the editor is the author's friend. Why should we count work on grant proposals that never were funded? This person's expertise in public libraries is irrelevant to their progress toward tenure in an academic library. That person was a member of my committee but never came to meetings. Then, the matter of collegiality would come up and the pitch of our chatter would rise to screeching heights.

Those meetings were a strange mix of Pandora's box, Kafka, and the *Gremlins* movies.[2] I thought of my junior colleagues, following the rules of that big manual as best they could, humbly soliciting what I had finally earned: job security, and the knowledge that their peers valued their work. What made us think we had the right to judge people in these terms? Hadn't we gotten beyond fraternity hazing? Many academic librarians are into their second or third careers and/or graduate degree(s) by the time they get to the promotion and tenure process. Could we not stipulate that we would not judge each other so harshly, just because we can?

Enforced Mediocrity

Of course, there is that other thing. Huh? Oh yes. The gremlins lower their voices when venturing into this territory. Professional jealousy ...? Can someone really be too good to fit in at our library? Yes, they can. This is probably the most distasteful thing that promotion and tenure committees ever do or ever encounter and they will most likely never admit it. Everyone involved in the process must fulfill certain criteria; everyone must follow the rules of the manuals and the cultural norms of the process as played out in each library and university. However, there are always colleagues who do more than their share in all of the categories. They write more articles, speak at more conferences, are elected to chair more committees, and just never seem to do anything but work and excel at it. Maybe they are really nice people too. They are most likely always busy. I hope that in our organizations, we would find ways to reward these people with early tenure and promotion, raises, or other merit recognition. Maybe people who excel in this way come across as distant and prickly to others.

The gremlins never seem to rest either, flitting around our heads, putting the "lacks collegiality" words into our mouths. It is hard to imagine that such super-achievers would not earn tenure, but if they received negative comments and do not feel valued, they may decide to take their energy and excellence elsewhere. This is not what the system intends to do, but it is what real people often do when enmeshed in such a system. We cannot ignore or get rid of the gremlins if we refuse to see them in the first place. The only way to keep from enforcing mediocrity is to acknowledge that it happens.

It's Not What You Say But...

I wonder sometimes about those right-wing conservative academics who struggle through academia feeling outnumbered and oppressed by their left-liberal colleagues who hate them. At the same time, they rail against the left-liberal-ethnic-gender-identity folks who struggle through the academic process feeling oppressed by all the white male conservative academics who *hate* them. What anybody on either side of the ideological spectrum should realize is that it doesn't matter *what* they think or write, just that they write *something* and get it published *somewhere* in a peer-reviewed journal or edited book and tote them all up on a vita, and, *Voila!*: tenure and promotion!

That other thing (you know, ideology) really doesn't matter, because most of the promotion and tenure guidelines I've seen require only that you leap some kind of quantitative hurdle in the publication and/or creative activity track meet. I know for a fact that deans like to use spreadsheets and tallies. They devise forms for this, they use them, and I have heard that they even *shred* them after they compare and contrast the accomplishments of their faculty. A person's record begins to look like a Chinese restaurant menu—so many dishes in column A for publications, a few more in column B for service ... You get the idea. Do you think deans actually *read* all that stuff before they decide where to put that tally mark? In my experience, peers on promotion and tenure committees are more likely than deans or other administrators to take an interest in the content of your publications, creative activities, and service. In practical terms, you can use this to your advantage by carefully highlighting the accomplishments that you feel are most important on your vita and in your dossier. If you want your colleagues to read your publications, provide extra copies for them. If your work has been recognized by citations in professional literature, or if your colleagues have told you of its usefulness, include a few "testimonials" to that effect in your documentation. This is the best way to show that your work makes a difference, and it may be the only thing that will give it more personality than that tally mark on the dean's spreadsheet.

A "Strange Little Town"

Most tenure systems enforce mediocrity—many people producing beans for the deans to count. But there is that rare possibility that something you write or say or do in the course of your professional life will make a discovery or state an opinion that gets the attention of some popular publication and then you get reprinted in the local paper and then you are noticed beyond the thin air of academe, down there where most people live and breathe. Newsworthy activities (and especially opinions) are not always convivial to those on Main Street, and this is when the principles of academic freedom come into play. Consider the recent case of Professor X from a small public university in an isolated region of a very large western state. He published a lengthy article for an esoteric journal, describing both the good and the bad of living and teaching in this little town. Professor X had spent more than ten years there, had earned tenure, and was an established, if a rather eccentric, member of the community. The article praised the climate, the landscape, the safe community and friendly people, the joy of earning a good salary in a depressed region, and the value of academic freedom. But he also wrote that his students and many of those same friendly townsfolk were, "appallingly ignorant, irrational, anti-intellectual, and just plain stupid." His descriptions went on to include such phrases as "some of the dumbest clods on the planet." He noted that his faculty colleagues were "mostly a waste of space."[3]

Since the article had appeared in a small-circulation magazine devoted to libertarian politics and published in another and faraway state, Professor X did not think it likely that his university colleagues and hometown folks would ever see it, but things turned out differently. Professor X received death threats, numerous denunciations appeared in local papers, and his property was vandalized. The university president got calls from donors and university supporters demanding that he fire Professor X, or step down as president, or get *himself* fired. However, Professor X is tenured and the president respects academic freedom and never considered firing him an option. Professor X comes across as a rather prickly character; it certainly shows considerable lack of manners to trash one's students, colleagues, and town. Nevertheless, academic freedom implies that you do not lose your job for politics or bad manners. The local Chamber of Commerce and many residents of the "strange little town" organized a parade featuring, among other things, the proud wearing of dunce caps and clodhoppers, in celebration of their love for their town. Some eventually credited Professor X for helping to "bring them together."

Gourmet Recipes or Not, You Gotta Eat

As anyone can see, I am a bit cynical about the promotion and tenure process for academic librarians. Some things I say in this essay might undercut other chapters in this book, not to mention irritate some colleagues and deans. In the grand scheme of things, most of these folks will never read it, know, or care about my critique of a process at which I have been (more or less) successful. They will not care about the content of this essay. What they will care about is that it is a "publication in an edited academic book in the field of librarianship" and that will look good on my vita. Coming at this particular time in my career, it may even push me right over the top of that ultimate hurdle: the promotion to Full Professor! Can you imagine? Of course, I must convince my friend and editor to put it in the book, a book filled with good and practical advice for librarians who want to be successful in academia.

Even though you might think I'm a cynic, the reality is that I am a true believer. One of my beliefs is that I will always try to do the best I can at any job I am given. As I read my promotion and tenure manual after those first few months on the job, I realized that I would need to get some stuff on that vita; it was part of doing a good job in an academic library. I decided that if I wrote a few things that got published in library newsletters, books, and maybe even a journal— well, that is what they really were interested in. Writing an article seemed so daunting. What I really enjoyed was spending days and nights on the Internet (it was not even the Web yet; it was ftp and gopher and e-mail lists) and searching for information about Latin America. Since I was a "Latin American Specialist" and since my library did not have much money to buy books and subscribe to journals, I wanted to figure out how to get information free on the Internet. So I started putting lists together of places where I had found useful stuff. Remember that there were no search engines at all then, much less something like Google that actually works. I talked about my lists at a local conference that, with my luck, also happened to be an international conference because I live on the U.S.–Mexico border. I put that on my vita. Around the same time, my boss showed me a library journal that was looking for lists of Internet resources in different subject areas. I typed up a new annotated version of the handout I had given to the folks at the conference and a few months later, I had an article in a national library journal. Because "Internet Resources in ..." was trendy in librarianship in the early 1990s, I took advantage of being in the right place at the right time. My own research interest was a "hot topic" in the profession. People in the library world and the international business world (remember, the NAFTA era also began in 1993) sent e-mails asking me to write articles and compile lists of resources for their journals and books and magazines. So, by the time I was ready to go for the big T (tenure!), I had a nice list of publications and conference presentations, all variations on a similar theme, but I did work hard at it.

Curiosity kept me going, and I believe curiosity is a main ingredient in the recipe for survival and success in the academic library world. You might call it essential to having the "right stuff," described in the *Dictionary of American Slang* as "the best human ingredients, such as fortitude and resolution," a phrase that first came into use in the mid-19th century.[4] The first time I noticed that designation, it was in the title of Tom Wolfe's book about the first U.S. astronauts, *The Right Stuff* [NY: Farrar, Strauss, and Giroux, 1979], also noted in the *Dictionary of American Slang*. Since then, the phrase has become such a cliché that I cannot even estimate how often it is used. What does this have to do with how to survive as an academic librarian? I think it has everything to do with it. Because, to be successful in anything, whether astronaut or academic librarian, you have to have the "right stuff." That is what peers on library and university promotion and tenure committees will look for. That is what you will need to have, and (perhaps more importantly) that is what you will need to be able to *show that you have.*

Having the right stuff cuts two ways. In addition to you having the right stuff for the academic library, the library where you work must have the right stuff for you. There are many reasons why one library/university would be a good match for your interests and talents while another would not. In my case, I wanted to concentrate on Latin American studies. There are several places where this specialty exists in academic librarianship, but I was attracted to my particular library because, in addition to working in this subject specialty, I could also live near the U.S.-Mexico border. Knowing myself, I knew that being in a particular place and really getting to know it would be important to me. Thus, after a few years at my library, I felt at home and so I was willing to make the effort required to jump through the tenure and promotion hoops, although I had to grit my teeth at times. Even after getting my wonderful continuous contract, I had to stifle many urges to scream at my colleagues (oops! I mean at the gremlins) on the promotion and tenure committee. I have had opportunities to work on various border issues beyond librarianship, and living in the region for a long time has lent credibility to my voice and to my work as information professional and scholar.

So, another ingredient of this right stuff is finding that thing that you really like to do and then channeling it into the kinds of academic "products" that become part of a successful vita—the kind that will get you tenure. If (unlike me) you are a good organizer of people, then you may be destined for leadership in committee work in a professional organization like the American Library Association or another group. This kind of service is so valuable to librarianship that it can lead to a successful bid for tenure even if you have not done much in the research and writing categories.

I became an academic librarian because after years of being a part-time graduate student, activist, and hippie traveler, I found myself an overeducated single parent, living in a depressed region of the country, with no prospects for earning much beyond minimum wage. I went back to my mentor from my very first student job at my undergraduate university library and asked for advice. I was lucky to get a paraprofessional job there, based on my experience. One day it dawned on me that my bosses earned way more than twice what I was earning and the only difference was that they had an MLS and I didn't. Two years later, I had the degree, my first professional job, an e-mail address, and the time to be curious and be paid for it. At that time, exploring the Internet was not part of any academic librarian's job description; two years later, many of us were publishing articles about it. Although I never was a "techie," I will always feel a little proud of being part of that small "elite" who wrote about the Internet in the early 1990s. I know that I can no longer keep up with the growth of Internet resources, although I do plan to continue to document those sites that provide good research information on Latin America. I totally missed the financial rewards of the dotcom boom, although I did predict that some things would never be commercially viable, especially in Latin America, long before the dotcom bust proved me right. My curiosity about online communication and the Internet helped me achieve a very valuable thing. I have a job that I like in a place that I call home and thanks to the academic promotion and tenure system, my son graduated from high school in the same town where he attended first grade.

Back to my old professor—anthropologist, mentor, and poet—and our e-mail exchange quoted in my prologue. Despite a growing list of book reviews in library journals, a few articles in conference proceedings and journals, invited presentations, and chapters in books, I am still proud of the poems that I published in esoteric magazines and journals. These creative works stayed on my vita through the years leading up to my formal application for tenure. My dean at the time knocked on my office door one day with friendly mentorish advice that maybe my poetry did not belong on my professional CV. I did not take his advice and I got tenure anyway. It is sort of like that one special ingredient that you throw into the dish and maybe forget to write down, or maybe it was just something sitting around the kitchen, like the dregs of that really good red wine, or that fresh herb that you planted in the garden one year that never grew back. In the years since I got tenure, I have published some essays and other nonacademic pieces that I feel tell certain truths that matter just as much as academic research. My advice is to find what it is that you really like to do that enables you to tell your own truth and express it through research, writing, teaching, or service. Keep looking for those unique (and even mysterious) ingredients and then you can write your own recipe for success. Put it on your vita. It all counts.

Endnotes

1. E-mail conversation between the author and Miles R. Oct. 2002, 23 Oct. 2002.
2. *Gremlins*, dir. Joe Dante, perf. Zach Galligan, Phoebe Cates and Hoyt Axton, Warner Brothers, 1984. A boy inadvertently breaks three important rules concerning his new pet and unleashes a horde of malevolently mischievous monsters on a small town. Plot outline from the Internet Movie Database, www.imdb.com/title/tt0087363
3. Lee Hockstader, "Is Texas Really a State of Mind? The Professor May Disagree," *Washington Post* 19 Feb. 2004, Final Ed.: A04. I purposefully left out the names and specific places of this event, but they are easy enough to find in the press. See also: Barbara Novovitch, "It's Home Stupid Home, But the 'Clods' Can Read," *New York Times* 17 Feb. 2004, Late Ed. Final: A10. Roy Hamric, "Libertarian Magazine Article Hot Topic of Gossip," *Desert-Mountain Times*. Available 29 Jan. 2004: www.dmtimes.net/blog/_archives/2004/1/29/17027.html. The original article that caused Professor X's trouble appeared in the January 2004 issue of the journal *Liberty* (circ. 10,000) and was entitled, "A Strange Little Town in Texas." I have been unable to locate an original copy of the article. Quotes from the professor's original article are as quoted in the *Washington Post*.
4. Robert L. Chapman, ed., *Dictionary of American Slang*, 3rd ed. New York: HarperCollins, 1995. 463.

CHAPTER 14

Moving to the Academy in Mid-Career—A Field Guide for the Experienced Librarian

Anna Gold

"The true university of these days is a collection of books."
—Thomas Carlyle

In a career that has recently passed the twenty-five year mark, I have made several career transitions during which I claimed, in interviews, that all libraries face substantially the same challenges. Whether they work in a 3-million volume research library, a 29-million volume national library, or a 2000-volume special library, I asserted with some confidence that library professionals face the same opportunities and challenges: from our competition, our users, and from the environment we share. We deal in increasing expectations, diminishing resources, and the unpredictable but always shifting technological loom on which our work is woven.

That may still be a defensible position in an interview, but it does not mean that all library careers are the same. Five years after making a mid-career switch from federal to university research libraries, I know that there are things about academic librarianship I wish I had understood before I made the switch. I want to prepare, inform, and encourage others who are considering a mid-career move into academic librarianship. Although I draw on my own experience, what follows also reflects the comments, discussions, and ideas of colleagues who have also made this mid-career transition.

Mutual Attraction

> The university is no longer a quiet place to teach and do scholarly work at a measured pace and contemplate the universe. It is big, complex, demanding, competitive, bureaucratic, and chronically short of money.[1]

All librarians have undergone a university experience, taking at least one undergraduate degree, and commonly one or more graduate degrees. As students, we were familiar with, and probably enjoyed, the world of academe. We may believe that returning to university life as librarians will allow us to continue and expand our experience as students. We may believe that returning to university life will let us play a new role, like faculty, by contributing to the intellectual life of a close-knit and dynamic community. We may enjoy the hubbub of youthful energy around us, the cycles of quarters and semesters marking out the calendar; the intelligence and intellectual ambition of academic colleagues; the idealism of knowing we're there more for the interest of the work, than the money it will afford; the pleasure and interest we derive from standing in the flow of that constant stream of extended intellectual community—books, journals, images, data—that pass through the sluiceway of our libraries.

Are we fully prepared to receive what we ask for? Today's academic libraries, like today's universities, are no utopian retreats—for administrators, faculty, or students. They are competitive, uncertain, complicated, political, and constantly under pressure. The salaries can be low, and because the salaries are low, the quality of life outside work can be correspondingly stressful. Then there's the daily stress of change: universities—and their libraries—are engaged almost universally in reinventing themselves and their relationship to the world, while trying to conserve the most critical elements of the academy's mission of scholarship and teaching. In this, universities and colleges are no refuge from the demands faced by the institutions of business or government.

Herein lies the good news for nonacademic librarians: university library recruiters are interested in recruiting nonacademic librarians. Why? Because as brothers and sisters from other library planets, we bring knowledge, experience, language, and values from other cultures. Recruiters are looking for qualities and experience that may be bred for intensively outside the academic environment: executive ability, discipline, independence, patience, resourcefulness, or entre-preneurial and business skills; experience in collaborations and part-nership, marketing and community involvement, or building databases and information systems. It is not that these skills are not found in a research library; they are the hallmarks of research library leaders. Nevertheless, the business, enterprise, or community orien-tation of other types of organizations may provide vivid experiences and values in these areas that stand out, and are attractive to research library recruiters.

"… and Members of the Academy"—What You (Don't) Know about Academic Culture

As students, we enjoyed a personal, but incomplete view of aca-demic culture. We saw its cyclical pressures; the camaraderie of fellow students; hard-fought academic competition; the vivid experiences of intense social learning: late nights, long weekends, longer vaca-tions; and, in the end, when GPAs were calculated and honors handed out, the diaspora that followed the rewards of individual accomplishment and distinction.

That is not the academy. As any faculty member can tell you, the academy does not revolve around its students, but its faculty. It reflects centuries of tradition rooted in the cultures of monasteries and cathedral communities, with strict hierarchies of authority and strongly held values of sacrifice, service, and consensus. Despite its best efforts, the academy is often unfriendly to family life. Its politics may frequently be liberal, but there are deeply conservative elements in academic life, notably in a tenure system that favors research dis-tinction over innovation and excellence in teaching.

Yet, the academy is changing. There is a growing emphasis on the development of university–industry entrepreneurial partnerships. A swelling demand for lifelong learning is changing the composition of the student body and residential models of campus (and library) services. Changes in technology and in student expectations are driv-ing a revolution both in pedagogy and in ways of delivering learning experiences.

A prospective academic librarian can learn a great deal about what it's like to live and work in academia today by perusing the *Chronicle of Higher Education*. Read the delightful columns of Ms. Mentor ("words of wisdom about academic culture," chronicle.com/jobs/ archive/advice/mentor.htm). Read the Information Technology section of the *Chronicle* or subscribe to their "Wired Campus" RSS feed. Read *Educause Review* (www.educause.edu/pub/er) to get an idea of just how big and pervasive academic IT issues are in the life of universities. To understand what academic life and careers are like today, see the list of books and other resources published by the University of Michigan's Career Center (www.cpp.umich.edu/students/gradservices/ academic/acadlib.htm).

"The Center of the University"—The Academic Library as Cathedral

> In a large university, there are as many deans and executive heads as there are schools and departments. Their relations to one another are intricate and periodic; in fact, "galaxy" is too loose a term: it is a planetarium of deans with the President of the University as a central sun. One can see eclipses, inner systems, and oppositions.[2]

For a long time, university libraries liked to describe themselves as being at the "center" of the university. They aspired to and often actually did occupy the largest, most beautiful building on campus. The whole notion of a centrally located library at the heart of a unified campus, culture, and community mirrors the great tradition of the cathedral. Cathedrals were built for the ages, with spaces for worship and ritual, places visited in order to receive the sacraments of knowledge, served by priestly communities of *cognoscenti* ready to administer sacraments and hear confessions. These images and ideas die hard, even while campuses spread like suburbs and libraries populate across sprawling landscapes with no single "main library." In other words, there are warring forces of centralization and distribution in most campuses, and they are reflected in most university libraries. There is virtue in both. If the cathedral model runs the risk of becoming "rigid, dogmatic, and insular, it also has an upside: a unified architecture, cohesive attitudes and approaches, strong motivations, and concentrated efforts." [3]

For a mid-career librarian considering the move to academe, it is important to be aware of the tension between central and diffuse models and of your own cultural biases and preferences. Regardless of what organizational model an academic library follows, what sustains the periphery while holding the center together is the human organization of the library. There may be no aspect of academic library culture more distinct from libraries in other sectors than the way it organizes people to do business.

The influence of traditional models of university organization can be found in many larger academic library organizations, most of which still bear some more or less strong vestiges of traditional hierarchy. Typically, a University Librarian, Director, or Dean of Libraries leads the library. A small number of high-level administrators form the highest executive's Cabinet, Council, or Steering Committee, who hold weekly, confidential meetings. The members of this second layer of power include administrators in charge of administrative operations (facilities, budget, and human resources), public services operations, collections and technical services, and information technology. These are Deputy Librarians, Associate University Librarians, Associate Directors, and the like. They are to the University Librarian as Deans are to the President of a university. It is common to find a layer of auxiliary high-level staff in this orbit: directors of development, digital initiatives, communications, or other library-wide functions with important roles dealing with campus at large, or with other libraries. Below these administrators are heads of library departments. They are high-level middle managers, with reports ranging from one to several libraries or functional units. Then there are the first-line managers, who may have one to half a dozen reports each, including highly experienced and skillful nonlibrarian assistants, who may themselves be supervisors or unit leaders. Then there are the committees, formed by the moons of this planetary system—the staff supervisors and department heads—pulling on the tides of the remaining staff in meeting after meeting like endless waves on the shore. Committees are established wherever services and functions require coordination across libraries; hence standing committees may exist to coordinate library operations such as reference, circulation, instruction, or collection development. There may be teams or advisory groups for course reserves, digital library development, Web services, interlibrary borrowing or lending. Umbrella groups may coordinate across the committees, through either staff representatives or managers or both. There may be sub-committees, councils, advisory groups, and teams. Most of these groups meet regularly, reporting their minutes to a wide distribution list or on the Web. If the library has a peer review process for evaluating tenure or promotion bids, there may be meetings to consider personnel matters. Recruitment of new staff involves bursts of intensive meeting activity. If a university is part of a consortium, there may be another layer of committees to support cooperative programs and special projects. In some libraries the amount of time spent in committee work may be so burdensome that a kind of gridlock takes place and work is *only* accomplished during meetings, never outside, because there is no outside. That's the worst case. A happier result is that there is never any lack of opportunity for a librarian to participate in system-wide work with peers from other departments. There are always more chances to demonstrate leadership and the ability to work with others than there are librarians to go around.

This is not to say that university libraries are not exploring other ways of organizing themselves: the University of Arizona Libraries are the canonical case of a library reorganizing its work around teams rather than functional hierarchies.[4] Whether work is accomplished in committees, teams, task forces, or working groups, be assured that any skill and experience you have working with groups and any demonstration of superb oral and written communication skills will be sought after and valued. Consulting with one's peers and success in consensus building are critical evidence that one has the collegial chops to make it in the academic jungle.

If you are a mid-career librarian you may well be coming into academic librarianship as a supervisor, and will need a special word of advice about your role in the hierarchy versus your role in committees. It is broadly assumed that members of a committee are equal in rank, regardless of their respective roles in the reporting hierarchy. Naturally, this means that work in committees is not "supervised." A team or committee may have a rotating chair, a facilitator, or a "leader," but that person has no supervisory control over the other members. At the same time, as a leader in a hierarchical system, you are expected to get things done. (This is quite different from the federal library sector, where operational and hierarchical leaders are generally the same people.) Like a Zen koan, this deep contradiction, built like warp and weft into the fabric of academic library organizations, is something on which you may meditate for the rest of your career:

A monk asked Tozan, "How can we escape the cold and heat?" Tozan replied, "Why not go where there is no cold and heat?" "Is there such a place?" the monk asked. Tozan commented, "When cold, be thoroughly cold; when hot, be hot through and through.[5]

With so much emphasis on equity and harmony amongst colleagues, in the academy there is nevertheless an irreducible element of competition in academic life. The playing field is not level. There are alliances, rivalries, histories, and legacies in the environment. You may land in a most-favored-nation type of department, or one that has always had trouble getting respect, or nice chairs for its students, or laptops for its librarians. You may feel you spend all your time trying to accomplish things in groups, but are still be expected to distinguish yourself as a leader or researcher when it comes to getting tenure or promotion. The luckiest, and wisest, academic librarians love what they do and like people. They will sidestep messy rivalries, develop a record of personal contribution to the profession, and be courteous and helpful to their colleagues. It is possible to do both. Remember Henry Kissinger's famous dictum about university politics—"University politics are vicious precisely because the stakes are so small"—and resolve to do better.

About those stakes. Some academic libraries are chronically under funded. Many academic librarians are, or feel, underpaid. The fortunes of most academic libraries are tied to the financial status of their parent institutions. These in turn are tied to the performance of investment portfolios, the economy, and the solvency of the state or local government they serve. They are large, but also fragile, dependent creatures. Well over half the budget of academic libraries is devoted to paying library staff. There are large, fixed costs of running facilities (usually going up) and the enormous cost of library collections (always going up). This means that staffing is usually where libraries can make regular savings.

Money is a big issue in libraries; few are independent of cyclical and environmental economic pressures. There are many ways for budget managers to handle this inevitable uncertainty, but it is not unusual for real budgets and expenses to be well-guarded mysteries. These mysteries may be honored through peculiar local customs—rites of spring such as spending out or carrying forward; there may be no rules constraining how things are paid for, or ironclad laws about spending across budget categories. Whatever the local rules may be, if you are going to be asked to develop or manage a budget, once you arrive, find out everything you can about it, including who has control over the kinds and amounts of spending. In bad budget years or good, if you can bring money into your part of the organization through grants and gifts, that can add significantly to your perceived, and actual, power to get things done.

Because money is important, if a position is being filled, the library has probably required a careful justification of its importance. The position may also have been vacant for a long time in order to accrue what is referred to as "salary savings." This means that when you are hired, you are wanted. However, it also may mean that others have been performing your work for some time. As welcome as new hands on deck may be, adjusting to your arrival may not be easy for those who have been doing your work.

If you join the staff of an academic library, you will also become aware of a constant drumbeat about change. Academic research libraries have deep roots and long memories, but there is no doubt in anyone's mind that the way they accomplish their mission is changing. Understanding change and knowing what it means to lead or manage change are essential tools of any mid-career professional. Understanding the capabilities of technology; accepting high levels of uncertainty; cultivating personal qualities of humor, imagination, persistence, and empathy; these are survival skills that will help get you through this dark night of the research library's soul.

What to Expect They're Expecting: Interviewing for the Mid-Career Move

The opportunity to hire a new librarian is an important community event in an academic family. Filling open positions usually requires substantial effort on the part of many members of the library staff: the administrator who justifies filling the position, the assistants who wrangle dozens of people's busy schedules and make travel and transportation arrangements for interviewees, and the dozens of committee members who deliberate for hours before and after your arrival to come up with just the right questions to ask you and to analyze your answers. For a government or special librarian, this may all seem a little strange, and it is useful to know in advance how different this process may be than your experience in other sectors. For example, whenever I have competed for a position in a federal library, the experience felt like something between taking a final exam and auditioning for a play. It was an intense experience but if one studied hard, knew one's lines, and had one's paper (resume and application) in order, things would go well, and it was over in an hour or so. In the unlikely event that your interviewers had extra time before the next candidate, you might get a tour of the facility.

In contrast, interviewing for a position in an academic library is like meeting your fiancée's family for the first time. It is grueling. It is sociable. You will need a bottle of water to get you through the day, and you will bless the few minutes you have to yourself in the restroom. There will be lunches and dinners. You will give a presentation in front of an assembly of other library staff. All of this means that competing for a job in an academic library requires you to prepare intensively and specifically for this particular job.

Unlike many federal and special library jobs, academic positions are widely advertised, usually nationally. Most jobs will be posted to appropriate library listservs. They will also be advertised in at least one print venue—often *College and Research Libraries News* or *Chronicle of Higher Education* (chronicle.com/jobs). Even when there are good internal candidates for a position, there is likely to be aggressive recruiting to fill mid-career vacancies. People will be on the lookout for credible candidates at national or regional conferences and they will call their friends and colleagues at other institutions to see if they have someone to recommend. The world of academic librarianship, as vast as it may seem to you coming from an independent special library, is still a small world. People know each other. They move from one library to another, they have connections and use them. It is not uncommon for libraries to raid each other's staff. As an outsider, you are likely to be a relative unknown.

How can you overcome this disadvantage? The most important thing you can do is to bone up on your target employer. If they have a library intranet (ask; it may require a password or knowledge of an obscure URL), spend as much time as you can afford reading through it to glean corporate history and hot issues, and to read through important reports and planning documents. The site may not be up-to-date, but it will be informative. Become familiar with major library projects and initiatives, the particular organization of committees and libraries. Spend time on the Web site of the parent institution. Try to get a feel for what makes this campus and college unique. What areas of research are booming? How are the finances of the organization? What changes are there in curriculum and degree options? Who runs campus information technology? What kind of courseware is in use?

The next most important thing you can do to strengthen your bid for an academic position is to highlight your transferable experience: your work on major projects, involvement in national professional activities, your research initiatives, or your management abilities—anything that demonstrates strong teamwork and leadership. Highlight your communication skills and inclusive decision-making practices. If you can, demonstrate during your interview or presentation the creativity and sense of humor that will make you a spirited and pleasant colleague.[6] And do not leave during lunch. Urban legends persist about interviewees who escaped the clutches of their handlers mid-day by hiding in the restaurant bathroom. Do not do this if you can possibly help yourself. Be prepared for a ten- to twelve-hour interview day.

If this seems extraordinary to you, remember that interview practices in most college and university libraries roughly follow time-honored practices used by academic departments when they hire new faculty. Their practices are not dissimilar to high-tech interviews at many corporate campuses. This means that your interview will be on site, following at least one round of telephone interviews. It will last at least a day and possibly a day and a half or more. Your day will begin early, around 8 A.M., and you will be ushered through half a dozen or more individual and group interview sessions. In between these, you will make a presentation before a group of library staff, and you will field questions from the audience. You will be taken out to lunch. You will be taken out to dinner. These are opportunities for you to relax and enjoy your potential colleagues, and for your colleagues to express their hospitality. Well—yes and no. These pleasantries are, as Clausewitz's said about war and politics, a continuation of your interview by other means. These people want a chance to sell you on their community (the great schools, where you can afford to buy a house, the fact that the weather is "never like this," or the unofficial rumors about raises you might get next year). In turn, they will glean what they can about the purity of your motives or your grace under what everyone knows is relentless pressure.

Put out a heroic effort, stay organized, and try to enjoy yourself. Be positive. Listen well to their questions, and answer them directly. Given a choice between being brief and "going long," be brief.[7] Be honest. With so many eyes and ears trained on you, you are unlikely to pull the wool over anyone's eyes—do not waste their time, or your own. They have put thought into the suggested presentation topic: Use it to launch into things you know and care about, but do not ignore it or meet it halfway, or your presentation, however interesting, will disappoint. Be comforted that whatever effort you put out, your interviewers are also being put through the wringer. Despite their own hectic schedules, they are devoting many hours to preparing for your interview. They are taking notes on what you say, and may have to write them up for your file. They will reflect on and discuss your answers, and debate your merits with generosity and sensitivity. After all that, if they ask you to join their enterprise, how can you refuse?

If you reach this point, be sure you get all the facts about your proposed salary, benefits, relocation reimbursement, or other assistance. Find out when you will be evaluated for promotions or raises. There is a lot of uncertainty in university budgets: the fact that the last ten years have seen cost of living increases each year doesn't guarantee you'll get one next year. If you are used to job offers in government, you may not realize how much room you, and your prospective employer, have to negotiate. If you can, tactfully ascertain how the offer they are making will position you in relation to your peers: people in similar positions, or with the same number of years in the profession. The first job offer you get is unlikely to be their "best and final offer." There is no harm in asking for what will make you happy and effective in the job, as long as you are not perceived as asking for special treatment ("about that vacation home in Aspen …"). Do you dislike your prospective job title and have a suggestion for something more accurate? Do you need a laptop to work efficiently? Tell them it would make you more productive to have a laptop. Ask what their laptop policy is. Do you need to attend more professional conferences than usual to make this job transition successfully? Ask for a temporary increase in your travel allowance and explain why it will benefit their organization. If you are a mid-career candidate for a hard-to-fill position, you may be able to get all or most of your moving expenses paid for. Do you need to finish out a school year in your current job for the sake of your kids? Ask. They may feel pressure to get you out there to participate in time-sensitive decisions or events, but maybe you can meet their needs via phone calls or another campus visit. With some exceptions, recruiters have some latitude in the package of salary, status, and benefits they can offer. They are not going to withdraw a job offer simply because you have asked for something they are unable to give you.

Like any immigrant from another culture, you may find making the move to the promised land makes more sense if you have some idea of the cultural and environmental differences you can expect in moving from your homeland. If you work in a government library, you are likely to find that salaries in academe are lower and raises less certain. You will probably earn more vacation time in academia, unless you have been in government service for many years. You will not have to show your ID or credentials every time you walk through the front door. You will probably not have to account for your time at work as rigidly as at many government agencies. If you are used to accomplishing your department's work by hiring knowledgeable and experienced consultants, this is likely to change if you move to academic librarianship. To bring in needed skills, you will have to develop existing staff or find skilled partners in other campus departments. Roles and responsibilities for staff in a government library may be more explicit but less flexible than those in academic libraries. Job descriptions in government libraries, if they are kept up to date, are comprehensive and prescriptive. In contrast, job descriptions in academic life tend to be fluid documents that are born as recruitment advertisements, and are modified from year to year as roles and priorities change.

If you are a corporate or industry librarian you may find the move to academe will bring you into a much broader community of peers. You are likely to earn less in academic work than in a corporate setting. On the other hand, your job's existence is likely to be more stable. You may experience a loss of independence and agility as you face the need to accomplish work through committees, networking, and consensus building.

What if you are already in the academy, but not yet a librarian? A new vocation in a library setting may appear to offer the best of all possible worlds: a stable career path, colleagues who appreciate your academic credentials, and the chance to continue your research and your involvement in the life of the intellectual community, without the pressures of publishing and tenure. While there is some validity to these expectations,[8]

> …those who turn to library science expecting a placid retreat from the job crisis in the humanities and a refuge from modernity are in for an unpleasant surprise. As a profession, library science is undergoing rapid change as new technologies throw the utility of older practices into question. [9]

Most academic librarians lead very busy lives with very little time to devote to research. Just as research faculty struggle with balancing the obligations of service (undergraduate teaching, advising, committee work) and research, so too do librarians. Academic librarians typically struggle to find balance between day-to-day demands of service, committees, supervision and management, and productive research and development. Relatively few academic librarians are engaged in long-term scholarly research programs, though many face real pressure to publish in order to gain promotion or tenure. Perhaps the answer to this dilemma lies in another koan:

> One day as Manjusri stood outside the gate, the Buddha called to him, "Manjusri, Manjusri, why do you not enter?" Manjusri replied, "I do not see myself as outside. Why enter?"

For these reasons perhaps (and with some exceptions) what counts as research in academic libraries is actually quite practical. It demonstrates your ability to engage in collective problem-solving and project development, and to draw and share lessons from experience.

The Heart of the Academy: Learning

> … A university's essential character is that of being a center of free inquiry and criticism—a thing not to be sacrificed for anything else.[10]

For a librarian who has spent a good part of his or her working life outside the academy, the siren song that lures them back is almost certainly their innate excitement about learning. Whatever else the modern university or college may be about, there is no denying that learning is the core activity of the academy. If they don't overwhelm the poor immigrant, the uncertainty and complexity of the academic library organization and mission offer opportunities for learning that are hard to surpass in any other library setting. Whether you join a small or large academic library organization, you become part of an "academy" of librarian colleagues who will look to you as a partner in both change and tradition. Your ability to keep on learning, and your willingness to share your newfound discoveries with your colleagues, is a sure ticket to personal satisfaction and professional respect in your new country.

Endnotes

1. Dain, Phyllis, in *Aspirations and Mentoring in an Academic Environment*, by Mary Niles Maack and Joanne Passet, "Commentary" section (1994). From a speech given at the 1990 annual conference of the Association for Library and Information Science Education.

2. Barzun, Jacques, *Teacher in America*, ch. 13, Little, Brown (1954).

3. Eunice, Jonathan, May 11, 1998, "Beyond the Cathedral, Beyond the Bazaar," www.illuminata.com/cgi-local/pub.cgi?docid=cathedral

4. Owens, Irene, "The Impact of Change from Hierarchy to Teams in Two Academic Libraries: Intended Results versus Actual Results Using Total Quality Management." *College and Research Libraries*, 60:6 (1999): 571–584. See also the University of Arizona list of teams, www.library. arizona. edu/library/teams/teams.html.

5. Zen Koans: Transcending Duality, www.chinapage.com/zen/koan1.html

6. For more insights into what college and university libraries look for in candidates before they let them into their family, ACRL posts a lengthy list of qualities ("What do employers want? Qualification keywords for library positions," www.ala.org/ala/acrlbucket/cls/acrlpresentation/2003 alapresentationqualifications.htm).

7. From the *Chronicle of Higher Education* comes this critical advice to candidates for faculty positions. It applies equally to positions in academic libraries: "The very few candidates who take my opening question as an invitation to solo for 30 minutes have made a fatal error. Our best interviews are, in fact, lively conversations, replete with turn-taking, stepping on other people's lines, back-tracking, false starts, digressions, and occasional thoughtful silences." Dennis Baron, "The Job Interview," January 21, 2001, *Chronicle of Higher Education* (chronicle.com/jobs/2002/01/ 2002012101c.htm).

8. "The library profession consistently offers a deeply satisfying career with multiple rewards that are too often missing from the faculty positions within reach for most Ph.D.'s. I'm talking about things like career mobility; faculty status; opportunities for advancement such as sabbaticals, release time to conduct research, and money to travel to conferences; not to mention a regular paycheck, generous benefits, and challenging, interesting work with books, electronic resources, and educated people." Todd Gilman, "Putting your PhD to work in libraries," *Chronicle of Higher Education*, April 8, 2004.

9. Bradley, Gwendolyn. "Careers in Academic Libraries." *Chronicle of Higher Education*, Friday, April 20, 2001.

10. Hofstadter, Richard. 1968 commencement address, quoted in "Parting Shots: A Century of Commencement Speeches," *Saturday Review*, May 12, 1979.

CHAPTER 15

A View From the Top—What the Director or Dean Is Looking For

Benjamin Wakashige and Emily Asch

*"James I of England once famously (and prophetically)
said, 'No bishops, no king.' I say, no administrators, no life
of the mind."*
                                        —Stanley Fish (1938-)

In response to changes brought on by demands of their customers and the integration of information technology, today's academic libraries focus their energy and resources on providing quality service as they strive to become the learning center of the academic community. As we enter a new millennium, academic libraries are challenged to address issues that have immediate impact on providing a program of excellence to their clientele. The ACRL's Focus on the Future Task Force in 2002 identified six major issues facing academic libraries: recruitment, education, and retention of librarians; role of the library in academic enterprise; impact of information technology on library services; creation, control, and preservation of digital resources; chaos in scholarly communication; support of new users; and higher education funding (Hisle, p. 714). Academic libraries need effective leadership to meet and address these challenges and to create an environment where the library is the learning center of the academic community.

Today's academic library director must effectively and efficiently manage the multitude of library processes and create a healthy and productive work environment. Library administrators should be proficient and knowledgeable in areas of human resources issues, budgeting, technology, planning, management, public relations, and fundraising. They also need to ensure library representation in the appropriate academic councils and committees, fight for scarce resources, and create a physical environment of learning and study. In addition they must be accountable to the library's clientele, be open to new methods and technology, provide leadership for change, motivate the staff, communicate effectively, and advocate for the library's program. At the same time, today's libraries demand attention, illustrated by Joe W. Hewitt's study of research libraries in which he identified the following organizational needs: organizational flexibility, stronger external and client-centered orientation, increased staff empowerment and work satisfaction, and improved management processes such as communication, coordination, and planning (Hewitt, p. 6).

Obviously, the role of the library director is varied and multifaceted. The director cannot do it all alone, but relies on the staff for the success of the campus library program. Library directors are looking for a staff that will get the job done in a positive and constructive manner and in a team environment. If you are to be a contributing member of the organization, where do you fit in? What can you do to help the organization become a more healthy and effective organization in these challenging times?

Personal Characteristics

A person's attitude toward his or her work is critical to the ultimate success of that individual, especially if they aspire to progress in their workplace and profession. Have a positive attitude about your work and coworkers, bring energy to the work, and be creative. Often the library director does not have a great deal of time to spend with individual librarians, particularly if the library has a large staff. Because of this, it is important to leave a positive first impression with the director. Go out of your way to initiate contact. Take a positive attitude with you; administrators are more receptive to employees who have a positive approach to their work. With all of the responsibilities and problems that administrators encounter on a daily basis, they appreciate those who have a good attitude. You will find that this positive approach to problems will lead to positive responses and improved communication. When bringing any situation to the attention of your supervisor(s), be prepared not only to describe the problems but also to suggest possible solutions.

Bring energy and enthusiasm to the workplace. This shows in the appearance of your workplace, dress, and actions. When selecting individuals for committees and new tasks, the director often seeks out librarians with energy and enthusiasm. Do not be afraid to be assertive. If there is an opportunity to volunteer and you feel that you can contribute to the situation, be proactive and volunteer. If the director has an "open door" policy, take the opportunity to go in and share suggestions on how the work and/or workplace could improve. Assist the library administration by examining and providing solutions to problems.

Being an effective contributing member of a team is critical as organizations increasingly move toward a team management program. This requires learning interpersonal skills that make you a good team player. As a member of the team, you are expected to be an active contributing participant and work toward common goals. The success of the team is not dependent on the work of one person, but on the collective contribution of all its members. Learn to work with your colleagues as part of a team.

The director wants someone who is hardworking and productive. Be willing to stay a little late or to take work home. Some people would argue against this, and it is often dependent on individual priorities and outside responsibilities. The adage "if you want something done in a timely and efficient manner give the job to a busy person" is often true. If you demonstrate to your director that you are hardworking and productive, perhaps you will get work that is more challenging. This will result in new skills and possibly promotion.

Have a passion for what you do. Remember why you decided to become a librarian; for many, it was to make a difference in people's lives. Do not lose sight of why you decided to enter the field. The passion for your vocation should show in your attitude and work.

Professional Qualities

The library director expects librarians to have the knowledge and ability to integrate technology into the workplace, to participate actively in planning processes, and to use problem-solving skills. The academic world must stay on top of quickly changing technology.

Without this knowledge of and continual learning about technology, an academic library cannot effectively serve the needs of students and faculty. Students continue to arrive at college with an increased knowledge of technology. Librarians must be able to address this issue and relate to students on the level of technology that they understand. Without this knowledge and willingness to learn continually, a librarian loses credibility and becomes ineffectual.

For an academic library to be effective and competitive, it is critical to view issues and plans in a strategic way. The demands of a changing environment require that the processes are responsive to rapid and sometimes unpredictable change. It is important that today's academic libraries be involved with strategic planning. The library staff must share a common vision, mission, and values as it moves forward. An effective library strategic plan is the result of total staff participation in the formulation process. You should take every opportunity to participate in strategic planning for the library and university.

Professional librarians should also take an active interest in learning new skills and taking leadership roles. With the rapid changes taking place in today's library, the need for training and staff development is becoming more important than ever. Without well-trained staff, a library will stagnate, leaving it unable to meet the needs of the academic community and the director unable to take it to the next level of service. Keep up with service trends, resources trends, and technology changes by participating in e-mail lists, by reading professional literature, and in other ways. There is a continual need for education; take the opportunity to attend workshops, seminars, and conferences. Participate in internship and leadership opportunities. Sign up for courses in areas where you feel you need more expertise and knowledge. After attending training and development activities, share what you have learned with your colleagues. Give a formal presentation, send out an informal report, or simply share the material distributed at the activity.

A dilemma faced by many academic librarians is whether to pursue a further advanced degree. The critical factor is whether a degree will further your professional career goals. If you want to become a library director or dean, then perhaps you should work toward a doctoral degree. The same would be true if you intend to go into library education. If you want to become more knowledgeable about an academic area, then perhaps you should pursue a second master's degree in a subject area. If a second master's degree is required for promotion or tenure purposes, or if your goal is to someday work at a library where you have full faculty status, by all means work toward that degree.

Projections of the "graying" of the library profession and the retirement of library administrators make the need for leadership development for librarians especially important. At the same time, the roles and responsibilities of library administrators are changing. New skills and knowledge are required in such areas as fundraising, grant writing, technology, and management. There is a call for a new kind of library director. Eric Shoaf identifies six attributes for tomorrow's academic library leaders: managing change, articulating a vision, knowing how to coach, living the service ethic, putting people first, and creating a culture of leadership (Shoaf, p. 365). If you are considering taking on an administrative job, you will probably have the opportunity at some point. If you are unsure of whether you are suited for or have the ability to lead, you should try out some administrative responsibilities. This could mean volunteering to serve as a chair of a committee or serving in an interim role when a supervisory vacancy occurs at your library. Attend workshops and conferences that address issues relating to library administration. Identify areas in which you need further development. These might include budgeting, fundraising, supervision, planning, or public speaking. Work toward becoming proficient in these areas. Review and keep up with the literature regarding leadership. For some academic librarians, the viability of relocating will be important when deciding to apply for an administrative position. There is no simple answer; everyone's situation is different. If you are considering a career move, ask yourself: Will it help me to achieve my long-range goals? Will it create new financial pressures? If relocation is necessary how will that affect my family?

Academia is not a 9-to-5 job. Students, faculty, and administrators work around the clock to complete their responsibilities and research. Likewise, the library staff must respond to meet the service needs of the academic community. Being a truly effective academic librarian who affects lives and the education of students and faculty is a mindset, a way of thinking. Providing good service means believing in what you are doing, and this may often mean working outside the eight-hour day. You have to be willing to do whatever it takes to get the job done. However, be sure that you have a clear understanding of your own personal priorities. If your personal health concerns or family life are higher priority, do not put work before those priorities.

To be an effective professional, you should first make an honest assessment of your skills that relate to your work. What are your strengths and weaknesses? What do you enjoy doing and what do you dislike? What skills do you have and what skills do you need to develop? After completing your assessment, identify the areas in which you need to improve. Develop a long-range plan on how you will address these issues. Perhaps you need to improve on your public speaking skills. Plan to take a public speaking course at a local community college or join the Toastmasters organization. If you need to become more proficient in strategic planning, you might sign up for a workshop on the topic or volunteer for the campus or library strategic planning team, if such an opportunity presents itself.

Service, Research, and Teaching

Generally, tenure and promotion requirements in an academic setting fall into four categories: *librarianship, service, research,* and *teaching.* If you are in a faculty status position, it is important that you expend your energies and time toward meeting these requirements. Your director will appreciate your efforts. Take the time to understand your institution's requirement and to plan your strategy for meeting the requirements.

Librarianship: Perform your job duties well. Be an active part of your library.

Service: Join and be active in your professional organization. Your involvement could result in networking, publication, presentation, and leadership opportunities. This could include your local, state, regional, and national organizations. You should direct your activities to organizations that assist you with meeting your service requirement. If you are a librarian in a large research university, involvement in a national professional association such as the American Library Association (including its divisions: ACRL, LAMA) or Special Library Association will probably be more meaningful for tenure and promotion than involvement in a local or state professional association. If you are interested in international librarianship, joining the International Federation of Library Associations (IFLA) might be a possibility. All professional organizations are looking for active members. Take the proactive position to contact the organization (usually the Vice-President Elect makes appointments) to volunteer for committee and task force assignments. Do not be afraid to volunteer for a leadership role within the organization. There are many leadership opportunities within professional associations. Make a point of attending meetings and conferences sponsored by the organization to demonstrate your interest and willingness to participate. Most organizations have publications that are looking for articles. Although they are generally not refereed (peer reviewed) publications, they could be listed in your vita. Through participation in an organization you will have the opportunity to meet librarians and to exchange ideas and information, which will enhance your work. Lifelong friendships and contacts develop through work in professional associations.

Become an active participant in library and on-campus committees and organizations. If there are committees that you are interested in joining, consult with your director and volunteer to serve on them. Be strategic in your selection of library committees. It is good to get out of the library and become involved in the larger campus community. Your involvement will not only contribute to the campus welfare, but will likely benefit your work performance as well. Student organizations are often looking for faculty and staff sponsors. Become involved in the community outside of your college or university. This could include joining service organizations such as Rotary International, Kiwanis, or Lions. It could also include becoming a public library board member, sports coach, or youth advisor.

Research: Research keeps the librarian on top of changes in the library world, brings recognition to the library and the college, and garners prestige for the librarian. Research activities often result in publications and conference presentations. Publications that you could participate in include book reviews, local, state, regional, and national professional publications, and professional journals. Often overlooked are in-house reports such as task force and committee reports. Authoring and editing in-house publications often takes more of your energy and time than writing articles for journals. Poster sessions at professional conferences are forums for presentation and documentation of research. Conference presentations are also venues for sharing research results. Grant proposals and grant reports are other forms of research documentation.

Teaching: Many academic librarians are involved in library education. This can include participation in the library's information literacy program; preparation of library Web pages, brochures, and handouts; serving at the information/reference desk or through virtual reference activities; and teaching in the classroom on campus or through a distance-learning program. Participation in library education activities is not limited to librarians in the public services areas. If you are in technical services, administration, or collection development, you can contribute to the information literacy program in many ways. You may also want to consider teaching subjects in which you have an advanced degree or expertise at your college/university.

Academic librarians and libraries will continue to encounter many challenges in the future. With the challenges come opportunities. Keep lines of communication open with your library director. Qualified librarians are needed to provide leadership and to take on the challenges for tomorrow's libraries. The retirement within the next decade of librarians in leadership positions intensifies this demand. If your career goal is to become an academic library director, prepare and position yourself to be ready for the challenge of library administration.

Works Cited

Hewitt, Joe A. "What's Wrong With Library Organization? Factors Leading to Restructuring in Research Libraries." *North Carolina Libraries*, 55 (1997): 3–6.

Hisle, W. Lee. "Top Issues Facing Academic Libraries." *College & Research Libraries News*, (2002): 714–715,730.

Shoaf, Eric C. "New Leadership for Libraries: Who has the Right Stuff?" *College and Research Libraries News*, (2004): 363–365, 375.

Stueart, Robert D., and Barbara B. Moran. *Library and Information Center Management*. Englewood, CO: Libraries Unlimited, Inc, 1998.

Afterword

"I must admit that I personally measure success in terms of the contributions an individual makes to her or his fellow human beings."
　　　　　　　　　　　　—Margaret Mead (1901–1978)

Higher education is always changing. Advances in information technology and distance education are just two among the many trends that will have critical impacts on our libraries in the future. There will, however, always be students and teachers, whatever form they may take, and they will always need information. As an academic librarian, you are in the best position to provide it.

In respect to the roles and characteristics of libraries and librarians, things may not change as fast as you think. Guy R. Lyle once said, "In the opinion of not a few, the tradition of the library as a storehouse of books and the librarian as a guardian of these books still clings like a millstone round the neck of the college librarian today.… Until this old parochial concept of librarianship is completely swept away by the entire goodwill and active support of college faculties, college librarians will continue to work under a distinct handicap in attempting to carry out the objectives of modern college librarianship."

Lyle wrote these words in 1944, and 60 years later we still sometimes experience this view of the academic library. However, you will have many opportunities to use your skills and knowledge in your chosen field. As an academic librarian, you are part of a tradition of preservation and dissemination of knowledge. It is a rewarding and challenging career in which you can perform a wide variety of tasks, from teaching and researching to contributing to the professional literature; from speaking and mentoring to creating unique information resources and new ways of learning.

In getting to know the academic librarians who contributed to this volume, one thing became very clear to me: They all love their work. I hope that, collectively, we have communicated this enthusiasm to you, and that the encouragement and advice you've found here will contribute to your success as an academic librarian. As you build your career, don't be overwhelmed. Take the time to enjoy life, your work, and your colleagues.

—Gwen Meyer Gregory

Works Cited

Lyle, Guy R. *The Administration of the College Library*. New York: H. W. Wilson, 1944.

Annotated Bibliography

These books, articles, and Web sites are recommended by contributors to *The Successful Academic Librarian*. They are the best resources we have found to help grow your academic career.

Library Careers

De La Peña McCook, Kathleen, and Margaret Myers. *Opportunities in Library and Information Science Careers*. Revised by Blythe Camenson. Chicago: VGM Career Books, 2001.

This handy little volume covers several areas of interest for the library job seeker: education requirements and job responsibilities, career placement for the new and mid-career professional, salaries and benefits, and future directions of the profession. Appendices include contact information for a good number of professional organizations, library schools, and professional journals.

Gordon, Rachel Singer. *The Librarian's Guide to Writing for Publication*. Lanham, MD: Scarecrow Press, 2004.

This is an excellent guide to all sorts of publication opportunities. Gordon takes you through the gamut of publication possibilities, from book reviews all the way to a whole book. Very encouraging and positive—the best book on the subject.

Info Career Trends. Edited by Rachel Singer Gordon. 2004. www. lisjobs.com/newsletter

Info Career Trends is a bi-monthly e-mail newsletter addressing career development topics. The focus is on practical advice for working professionals. Past themes have included continuing education, professional communication, mentoring and networking, balancing career and family, and professional associations.

Nesbeitt, Sarah L., and Rachel Singer Gordon. *The Information Professional's Guide to Career Development Online*. Medford, NJ: Information Today, Inc., 2002.

This practical guide goes beyond basic online job searching to discuss online current awareness resources, networking, listservs, professional associations, distance education, blogs and Web pages, and professional literature. A companion Web site, www.lisjobs.com/careerdev, offers an updated list of the links included in the book.

Pantry, Sheila, and Peter Griffiths. *Your Essential Guide to Career Success*. 2nd ed. London: Facet, 2003.

This volume is from *The Successful LIS Professional Series*. While it is British in focus, most of its content can be generalized to the U.S. experience. It contains explorations of various facets of career development and job hunting—analyzing the current market, developing a career plan, applying, interviewing, and others.

Shontz, Priscilla K. *Jump Start Your Career in Library and Information Science*. Lanham, MD: Scarecrow Press, 2002.

Shontz has compiled this book on many career development topics—job searching, networking, mentoring, publishing, etc.—updated with ideas and approaches relevant to Nexgen librarians. The book is peppered with advice and quotes that Shontz gleaned from dozens of librarians through interviews, questionnaires, conversation, and correspondence over a two-year period.

Siess, Judith A. *Time Management, Planning and Prioritization for Librarians*. Lanham, MD: Scarecrow Press, 2002.

Time Management, Planning and Prioritization for Librarians is simply a great help for all librarians.

Thomas, Joy, Ed. "The Role of Professional Associations." Special issue of *Library Trends* 46.2 (1997).

This article explores a variety of topics related to professional associations, including membership decisions, leadership benefits, virtual associations, paraprofessional membership, ethnic library associations, and associations at the international and state/regional levels.

Academic Libraries

Brown, Sally, Bill Downey, and Phil Race. *500 Tips for Academic Librarians.* London: Lib. Assn., 1997.

Succinct and interesting, this book gives short tips on handling work in an academic library. It is intended to be a tool for new librarians to learn their job, and to give more experienced librarians new ideas for their work. Advice covers topics such as managing the collection, supporting students, training staff, and professional development. British in focus.

Cubberley, Carol. *Tenure and Promotion for Academic librarians.* Jefferson, N.C.: McFarland, 1996.

Specifically aimed at librarians in faculty status positions, this book shares insights about how to work within the system effectively and succeed.

Hill, Janet Swan. "Wearing Our Own Clothes: Librarians as Faculty." *Journal of Academic Librarianship,* May 1994. 72–76.

Hill explains why it is important for academic librarians to articulate those special characteristics that determine how librarianship is practiced, as well as the standards of excellence by which its practitioners should be judged.

Hoggan, Danielle Bodrero. "Faculty Status for Librarians in Higher Education." *Portal: Libraries and the Academy,* 3.3 (2003): 431–445.

Hoggan presents the pros and cons of faculty status for academic librarianship in the form of a review of the literature. Her goal is to help individual librarians decide whether a faculty appointment is the right choice for them.

Hovekamp, Tina. "Work Values among Professional Employees in Union and Nonunion Research Library Institutions," *Journal of Applied Social Psychology,* 24 (June 1994): 981–993.

This article explores the relationship between unions and professional librarians' work values. Despite previous research findings on blue-collar workers, this investigation found no significant differences in the work values of professionals in unionized versus nonunionized libraries. However, differences in work-related values were traced when the present research looked just at the union group of the study. Data analysis indicated that registered union members and those most committed to their union placed higher degree of importance on professional growth issues than did their counterparts.

Shontz, Priscilla K., and Jeffrey S. Bullington. "Tips for New Librarians: What to Know in the First Year of a Tenure-Track Position." *College & Research Libraries News*, 59.2 (1998): 85–88.

This brief, easy-to-read article offers a number of helpful tips for the new tenure track librarian. The authors emphasize the importance of learning the job, work environment, and tenure expectations before tackling the research and service requirements. Advice ranges from the broad ("start networking") to the specific ("carry business cards").

Singleton, Brett. "Entering Academic Librarianship: Tips for Library School Students." *College & Research Libraries News*, 64.2 (2003):84–86.

This brief article highlights three areas of concern for potential academic librarians: professional assignment, professional development (including research), and service. It offers concrete suggestions on how to become familiar with each area.

Vesper, Virginia, and Gloria Kelley. *Criteria for Promotion and Tenure for Academic Librarians*. Chicago: Association of College and Research Libraries, 1997.

This resource includes results of a survey of 195 academic libraries. The survey, conducted in 1994/1995, gathered data about the academic status, promotion, tenure, rank, and other job status measures of academic librarians. The results are presented, as well as samples of tenure and promotion documents from a variety of institutions. There is no more recent comparable book.

Canadian Libraries

8Rs Research Team. *Future of Heritage Work in Canada (DRAFT)*. Edmonton: University of Alberta, 2004. Available 19 May 2004: www.cdncouncilarchives.ca/events/8RsFutureofHeritageWorkDRAFT. pdf

This valuable report (to be finalized in 2005) provides an in-depth review of the human resource issues facing libraries, archives, and museums in Canada. Each sector is presented separately in the report and the library section usually reports separate data for each of the three main library types—academic, public, and special. The section on libraries covers hiring; job market; future librarian demand for each of academic, public, and special libraries; retention; job satisfaction; mobility; salaries; and restructuring of organizations and of librarians' roles.

Leckie, Gloria J., and Jim Brett. "Job Satisfaction of Canadian University Librarians: A National Survey." *College and Research Libraries*, 58.1 (1997): 1–17.

This 1997 study of Canadian academic librarians' job satisfaction is a Canadian replication of a 1993 U.S. survey. It covers the topics of faculty status, administration, participation of librarians in planning, university affairs, workload, salary, and professional activities. A very valuable document for comparing and contrasting Canadian and U.S. academic libraries; the issues covered are still highly relevant today.

Noel, Wanda. *Copyright Guide for Canadian Libraries*. Ottawa: Canadian Library Association, 1999.

Wanda Noel's trusty copyright guide covers copyright issues for Canadian libraries. It begins with explanations of copyright in Canada and how foreign works are protected, including differences between U.S. and Canadian copyright. It provides a 13-page frequently asked questions section dealing with common copyright dilemmas and includes the complete Canadian Copyright Act and regulations from the Canada Gazette pertaining to book importation and exceptions for educational institutions, libraries, archives, and museums.

General Careers

Cohen, Norman H. *The Manager's Pocket Guide to Effective Mentoring*. Amherst, MA: HRD Press, 1999.

This small volume presents practical advice for the mentor to consider in establishing and maintaining the mentoring relationship. It explores six dimensions, or role purposes, of the mentoring process (relationship, informative, facilitative, confrontive, mentor model, and employee vision) and offers suggested behaviors and discussion angles to pursue for each dimension.

Cohen, Norman H. *The Mentee's Guide to Mentoring*. Amherst, MA: HRD Press, 1999.

This practical tool is designed to help the mentee understand both the mentoring process and his or her responsibilities in that process. In addition to exploring Cohen's six dimensions from the mentee's perspective, this work gives general guidance for selecting a mentor and maximizing the effectiveness of the mentoring experience.

Liebling, A. J. *The Earl of Louisiana*. Baton Rouge: Louisiana State University Press, 1970.

In 1959, press critic, war correspondent, food writer, and boxing aficionado A. J.Liebling blazed a trail across Louisiana for the *New Yorker* to chronicle Earl K. Long's last campaign for governor. Recommended to academic librarian colleagues because it is about the sheer enjoyment of the work one is given to do. The governor and the writer rollick together over back roads, through piney woods, swamps, and the smoke-filled rooms of political power in the "Gret Stet." You never doubt for a minute that they want to be anywhere other than where they are, doing exactly what they are doing at that very moment. There are passages to keep in mind as you tread the minefield (or paddle the swamps) of campus politics: "The bayous parallel the road on either side like stagnant, weed-strangled ditches, but their life is discreetly sub-surface—snapping turtles, garfish, water moccasins, and alligators. The mammals are water rats and muskrats and nutria, a third kind of rat. The nutria, particularly ferocious, is expropriating the other rats. Bird life, on the day we drove through, was a patrol of turkey buzzards looking down for rat cadavers. It was an ideal setting for talk about politics."

Shea, Gordon F. *Making the Most of Being Mentored: How to Grow from a Mentoring Partnership*. Menlo Park, CA: Crisp Learning, 1999.

Shea has five objectives: to explore the benefits of mentoring, to discuss the responsibilities of mentees, to explain the skills needed for successful mentoring, to provide guidance for productive mentoring relationships, and to identify techniques for maximizing results. The book uses a workbook format with exercises to aid the mentee in working through each area.

About the Contributors

Emily Asch is Cataloging/Technical Systems Librarian at the Harvey W. Scott Memorial Library of Pacific University, located in Forest Grove, Oregon. She received her library science degree in 2002 from the University of Illinois at Urbana-Champaign. She has previously worked in a public library and historical societies.

Wendy Baia is Head of Serials Cataloging and Interim Head of Cataloging at the University of Colorado at Boulder. She has 30 years of technical services experience in academic libraries, including the University of Michigan and Syracuse University. She has given local, state, and national presentations promoting user-friendly cataloging.

Joan Beam is Professor in Reference Services at Morgan Library of Colorado State University. Previously she worked in special and public libraries in Colorado and Iowa. She is the co-author of two books on Native Americans in fiction and the author or co-author of several articles in journals including *Serials Review, Journal of Academic Librarianship*, and *Reference Services Review*.

Nancy Sosna Bohm is Reference Librarian at Lake Forest College, north of Chicago. Previously she was a cataloging assistant at the College of the Siskiyous in northern California and Librarian at a college preparatory school in Sacramento, where she was responsible for circulation, cataloging, reference, and instruction.

Karl Bridges is Coordinator of Electronic Resources and Associate Professor in the Information and Instruction Services Department of the University of Vermont Library in Burlington, Vermont. Previously he worked at academic libraries in the Midwest. He is the author of numerous publications on library technology and personnel management. Educated in both England and America, he is a classicist and historian and is currently researching a new book.

Mary Beth Chambers is Catalog/Archives Librarian and Assistant Professor at the Kraemer Family Library at the University of Colorado at Colorado Springs. Previously she worked as a catalog librarian at the Cline Library at Northern Arizona University. She has co-authored several articles for publications including *Serials Review, Library Hi Tech,* and *Colorado Libraries.*

Cathy Cranston is Assistant Professor in Reference Services at Colorado State University Libraries. She received her B.A. in Anthropology from the University of Northern Iowa and her M.A. in Library Science from the University of Iowa. Currently she is the liaison to the Foreign Languages & Literature and Library Science faculty.

Anna Gold is Head of the Engineering and Science Libraries at the Massachusetts Institute of Technology. She was previously Head of the Science and Engineering Library at the University of California, San Diego. She has also worked in several federal libraries, including the National Science Foundation and the Library of Congress. She has written articles appearing in *Portal, C&RL News,* and the *Proceedings of the Joint Conference on Digital Libraries.*

Tina Maragou Hovekamp is Public Services Coordinator/ Associate Professor at Central Oregon Community College. Her doctoral dissertation at the University of North Carolina at Chapel Hill was her first attempt to study unions in academic libraries. She has published articles in a number of journals including *Library Trends, College & Research Libraries,* and the *Journal of Applied Social Psychology.*

Elizabeth O. Hutchins is a library consultant and educator. She was previously Assistant Professor and Coordinator of Library Instruction at St. Olaf College, and has also served as the library director at several independent schools in Massachusetts and a consultant to the Ministry of Education in Singapore. She has published articles/book chapters and offered workshops on library–faculty collaboration, information literacy, teaching/learning styles, and peer coaching.

Michelle Mach was Digital Projects Librarian at Colorado State University for six and a half years. Her articles have appeared in *Computers in Libraries, College & Research Libraries*, and other publications. Her service activities included LITA committee membership, academic advising, and Web site design for an honors organization. In 2003, the Colorado State University Office of Black Student Services awarded her the Special Friend Award for her service. Michelle currently works for a small publishing company in Colorado.

Rebecca Miller is Reference Librarian at the Donnelley and Lee Library of Lake Forest College near Chicago. She received her library science degree in 2001 from the University of Illinois at Urbana-Champaign, where she also worked as a graduate assistant. She worked in public and academic libraries in Boise, Idaho. She is an active member on ACRL committees, and has presented at conferences on information literacy.

Molly E. Molloy is Reference and Research Librarian for Border and Latin American Studies at New Mexico State University in Las Cruces. She has also worked at the University of Florida and at various paraprofessional jobs in libraries and in immigration law offices and as a translator.

Verla J. Peterson is Dean of Library Services at City University in Bellevue, Washington. She previously served as Assistant/Acting Director at Thomas Branigan Memorial Library in Las Cruces, New Mexico, and at academic and law libraries in Texas, Puerto Rico, and Wisconsin. Her professional interests include organization development, promoting leadership skills in the next generation of library professionals, and gender roles in librarianship.

McKinley Sielaff is Government Documents Librarian at the Tutt Library of Colorado College. She earned her MLS at Rutgers University and a Master of Public Administration at the University of Wyoming where she also received tenure as a library faculty member. She has also worked in a variety of public, special, and academic libraries.

Kris Swank is a librarian and adjunct instructor at Pima Community College in Tucson, Arizona, and proprietor of Swank

Research. Previously, she was a librarian at the American Graduate School of International Management (Thunderbird), in Glendale, Arizona, where she earned an M.B.A. in International Management. She has an M.L.S. from the University of Arizona. She has worked and traveled around the world.

Don Taylor is Electronic Resources Librarian at Simon Fraser University Library in Burnaby, BC, Canada. His previous position was Librarian for Reference and Resource Development at the former Technical University of British Columbia. His interest in the contrasts between U.S. and Canadian academic libraries stems from the two years he spent as the reference and liaison librarian for Engineering and Physical Science at New Mexico State University.

Benjamin Wakashige is University Librarian/Director of the Library at the Harvey W. Scott Memorial Library, Pacific University located in Forest Grove, Oregon. He has served as the New Mexico State Librarian/Director of the New Mexico State Library and as Library Director at Texas A&M University—Corpus Christi, Western New Mexico University, and the University of Albuquerque.

About the Editor

Gwen Meyer Gregory is Head of Bibliographic Services at the Tutt Library of Colorado College in Colorado Springs, Colorado. She was previously Associate Professor and Head of Bibliographic Services at New Mexico State University, where she also served as interim associate dean. She has worked in other academic and special libraries, doing everything from reference to instruction to preservation to cataloging. Her work has been published in journals including *Information Today, American Libraries, Public Libraries*, and *Technical Services Quarterly*. She is active in library organizations including REFORMA: the National Association to Promote Library and Information Services to Latinos and the Spanish-speaking, for which she is currently co-chair of the Recruitment and Mentoring Committee. She holds a BA in Anthropology from the University of New Mexico, an MLS from the University of Arizona, and a Master of Public Administration from New Mexico State University. She lives in Colorado Springs with her husband, Don Meyer, and their pug, T.C.

Index

More Titles of Interest from Information Today, Inc.

The Accidental Library Manager

By Rachel Singer Gordon

In *The Accidental Library Manager*, author Rachel Singer Gordon provides support and background for new managers, aspiring managers, and those who find themselves in unexpected management roles. Gordon fills in the gaps left by brief and overly theoretical library school coursework, showing library managers how to be more effective in their positions and how to think about their work in terms of the goals of their larger institutions. Included are insights from working library managers at different levels and in various types of libraries, addressing a wide range of management issues and situations. This readable and reassuring guide is a must for any librarian who wishes to succeed in a management position.

384 pp/softbound/ISBN 1-57387-210-5 • $29.50

Best Technology Practices in Higher Education

Edited by Les Lloyd

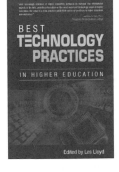

A handful of progressive teachers and administrators are integrating technology in new and creative ways at their colleges and universities, raising the bar for all schools. In his latest book, editor Les Lloyd (*Teaching with Technology*) has sought out the most innovative and practical examples in a range of key application areas, bringing together more than 30 technology leaders to share their success stories. The book's 18 chapters include firsthand accounts of school technology projects that have transformed classrooms, services, and administrative operations. The four major sections are "Best Practices in Teaching and Course Delivery," "Best Practices in Administrative Operations," "Technical or Integrative Best Practices," and "Future Best Practices."

256 pp/hardbound/ISBN 1-57387-208-3 • $39.50

Theories of Information Behavior

Edited by Karen E. Fisher, Sanda Erdelez, and Lynne (E. F.) McKechnie

Here are authoritative overviews of more than 70 conceptual frameworks for understanding how people seek, manage, share, and use information in different contexts. Covering both established and newly proposed theories of information behavior, the book includes contributions from 85 scholars from 10 countries. Theory descriptions cover origins, propositions, methodological implications, usage, and links to related theories.

456 pp/hardbound/ISBN 1-57387-230-X • $49.50

Understanding and Communicating Social Informatics

A Framework for Studying and Teaching the Human Contexts of Information and Communication Technologies

By Rob Kling, Howard Rosenbaum, and Steve Sawyer

Here is a sustained investigation into the human contexts of information and communication technologies (ICTs), covering both research and theory. The authors demonstrate that the design, adoption, and use of ICTs are deeply connected to people's actions as well as to the environments in which ICTs are used. They offer a pragmatic overview of social informatics, articulating its fundamental ideas for specific audiences and presenting important research findings.

240 pp/hardbound/ISBN 1-57387-228-8 • $39.50

Covert and Overt

Recollecting and Connecting Intelligence Service and Information Science

Edited by Robert V. Williams and Ben-Ami Lipetz

This book explores the historical relationships between covert intelligence work and information/computer science. It first examines the pivotal strides to utilize technology to gather and disseminate government/military intelligence during WWII. Next, it traces the evolution of the relationship between spymasters, computers, and systems developers through the years of the Cold War.

276 pp/hardbound/ISBN 1-57387-234-2 • $49.50

ASIS&T Thesaurus of Information Science, Technology, and Librarianship, Third Edition

Edited by Alice Redmond-Neal and Marjorie M. K. Hlava

The *ASIST Thesaurus* is the authoritative reference to the terminology of information science, technology, and librarianship. This updated third edition is an essential resource for indexers, researchers, scholars, students, and practitioners. An optional CD-ROM includes all terms referenced in the print thesaurus along with Data Harmony's Thesaurus Master software. In addition to powerful search and display features, the CD-ROM allows users to add, change, and delete terms, and to learn the basics of thesaurus construction while exploring the vocabulary of library and information science and technology.

Book with CD-ROM: 272pp/softbound/ISBN 1-57387-244-X • $79.95

Book only: 272pp/softbound/ISBN 1-57387-243-1 • $49.95

Net Effects
How Librarians Can Manage the Unintended Consequences of the Internet

Edited by Marylaine Block

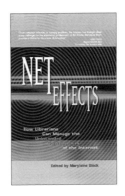

The Internet is a mixed blessing for libraries and librarians. On the one hand, it provides opportunities to add services and expand collections; on the other, it has increased user expectations and contributed to techno stress. Today, the Net is challenging librarians' ability to select, threatening the survival of the book, necessitating continuous retraining, presenting new problems of access and preservation, putting new demands on budgets, and embroiling information professionals in legal controversies.

In *Net Effects*, Marylaine Block examines the issues and brings together a wealth of insights, war stories, and solutions. Nearly 50 articles by dozens of imaginative librarians—expertly selected, annotated, and integrated by the editor—suggest practical and creative ways to deal with the range of Internet "side effects," regain control of the library, and avoid being blindsided by technology again.

400 pp/hardbound/ISBN 1-57387-171-0 • $39.50

The Information Professional's Guide to Career Development Online

By Sarah L. Nesbeitt and Rachel Singer Gordon

This book is designed to meet the needs of librarians interested in using online tools to advance their careers. It offers practical advice on topics ranging from current awareness services and personal Web pages to distance education, electronic resumes, and online job searches. New librarians will learn how to use the Internet to research education opportunities, and experienced info pros will learn ways to network through online conferences and discussion lists. Supported by a Web page.

416 pp/softbound/ISBN 1-57387-124-9 • $29.50

The Accidental Webmaster

By Julie M. Still

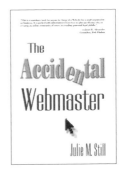

Here is a lifeline for the individual who has not been trained as a Webmaster, but who—whether by choice or under duress—has become one nonetheless. While most Webmastering books focus on programming and related technical issues, *The Accidental Webmaster* helps readers deal with the full range of challenges they face on the job. Author, librarian, and accidental Webmaster Julie Still offers advice on getting started, setting policies, working with ISPs, designing home pages, selecting content, drawing site traffic, gaining user feedback, fundraising, avoiding copyright problems, and much more.

208 pp/softbound/ISBN 1-57387-164-8 • $29.50

The Web Library
Building a World Class Personal Library with Free Web Resources

By Nicholas G. Tomaiuolo
Edited by Barbara Quint

With this remarkable, eye-opening book and its companion Web site, Nicholas G. (Nick) Tomaiuolo shows how anyone can create a comprehensive personal library using no-cost Web resources. If you were to calculate the expense of purchasing the hundreds of print and fee-based electronic publications that are available for free with "The Web Library," you'd quickly recognize the potential of this book to save you thousands, if not millions, of dollars (fortunately, Nick does the calculating for you!). This is an easy-to-use guide, with chapters organized into sections corresponding to departments in a physical library. *The Web Library* provides a wealth of URLs and examples of free material you can start using right away, but, best of all, it offers techniques for finding and collecting new content as the Web evolves. Start building your personal Web library today!

440 pp/softbound/ISBN 0-910965-67-6 • $29.95

The Extreme Searcher's Internet Handbook
A Guide for the Serious Searcher

By Randolph Hock

The Extreme Searcher's Internet Handbook is the essential guide for anyone who uses the Internet for research—librarians, teachers, students, writers, business professionals, and others who need to search the Web proficiently. Award-winning writer and Internet trainer Randolph "Ran" Hock covers strategies and tools (including search engines, directories, and portals) for all major areas of Internet content. Readers with little to moderate searching experience will appreciate the helpful, easy-to-follow advice, while experienced searchers will discover a wealth of new ideas, techniques, and resources. Anyone who teaches the Internet will find this book indispensable.

As a reader bonus, the author maintains "The Extreme Searcher's Web Page" featuring links, updates, news, and much more. It's the ideal starting place for any Web search.

296 pp/softbound/ISBN 0-910965-68-4 • $24.95

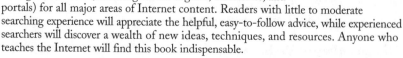

To order or for a complete catalog, contact:

Information Today, Inc.
143 Old Marlton Pike, Medford, NJ 08055 • 609/654-6266
email: custserv@infotoday.com • Web site: www.infotoday.com